NARROW

MW01680302

NOTES ON

IDENTITY

Discovering Who You Really Are

BILL SPENCER

– NARROW GATE –

Narrow Gate Notes on Identity: Discovering Who You Really Are. Copyright ©
2024 Narrow Gate Foundation. All rights reserved.

Narrow Gate Foundation
P.O. Box 267
Duck River, TN 38454

All Scripture quotations, unless otherwise indicated, are taken from the New King James Version®. Copyright © 1982 by Thomas Nelson. Used by permission. All rights reserved.

Scripture quotations marked NIV are taken from the Holy Bible, New International Version®, NIV® Copyright ©1973, 1978, 1984, 2011 by Biblica, Inc.® Used by permission. All rights reserved worldwide.

ISBN: 979-8-9868505-4-2

Printed in Canada

Table of Contents

Foreword

Why? I suppose that's a good question to begin with. Generations of theologians have written innumerable books containing invaluable insights into the mysteries of Scripture. Why would anyone want to pick up this little book? It's not the work of an accredited theologian who has spent a lifetime in the halls of academia gleaning wisdom and insight from heralded scholars. So, "Why" seems to be a fair question. Unfortunately, the answer isn't really all that remarkable.

For starters, thoughts move in and out of my head fast enough that if I don't write them down, I'll forget them (maybe you can relate). So, I take notes. To be fair, I rarely go back and *study* those notes. Sure, I refer to them from time to time, but I don't really *study* them, as if I'm preparing for an exam. I was always terrible at that sort of thing anyway. But I find that if I take notes and organize my thoughts while working through Scripture, the picture of my conversation with God becomes clearer. If I simply read and think, my mind drifts, and I rarely come to any clarified understanding that I can share with someone else. And isn't that the point of studying Scripture? To ingest something so deeply that its existence within you not only nourishes you but also gives you something to pass along to others?

The title of this book is fairly accurate. Not *The Mysteries Revealed* or *A Theological Commentary*. Instead, this is just a book of notes from one person who decided to write down what he saw as he studied his way through the text. But that still doesn't fully answer the question of why *you* are holding this book.

This book is far more than a record of *my notes* or *thoughts*. As you leaf through the pages, you'll notice that many of them are lined but not filled, and they have the heading "My Notes." These pages are the reasons why you're holding this book. Those pages are for you.

The notes contained in the book aren't designed to share insights that can't easily be found in multiple study resources. Rather, they are designed to get you to think and talk with God about His timeless and perfect expression of love toward you. The lined pages are interspersed with the populated ones, so you can record *your notes*. That's really the point of this exercise. It's not for you to learn what someone else thinks or knows; it's for you to record what you think and know. The notes are simply a primer for conversations between you and God. And that conversation is what truly matters.

As you record your thoughts, observations, insights, questions, and answers, you'll begin to connect more deeply with the text than you ever have before. And as you discover things for yourself, you'll have something to share with the people you encounter. That's the purpose of this book. You'll probably even notice, as you read through the pages that follow, that the recorded notes sound more like a discussion than observations. That's because I use my notes as a space where I can exercise how I'll share the insights of my study with the people I'll encounter. I'm not suggesting you should do the same, but it's a practice that has served me well for several years.

At Narrow Gate, where I spend the majority of my time, we're fond of saying, "Discovered truth is always more powerful than delivered truth." Here's your chance to discover truth that you can carry in your soul and share with others for the rest of your life. Here's a chance for the words and thoughts of God to become *your* words and thoughts. When that happens, you'll begin to notice how the words of God migrate into your daily conversations. You'll find yourself discovering how the struggles of life from thousands of years in the past are still present with us today. You'll build a compass of unchanging truth that will help you navigate the journey of our days from now until we see God face to face.

In short, if you'll take the time to compile your notes—your conversations with God about His timeless truth—you'll be changed into a vessel of loving compassion that can be used to rescue and transform others. And that is a good answer to the question, "Why?"

So, let's get started.

Introduction

A young woman once asked an artist, "Of all the pieces you've created, which is your favorite?" The artist thought for a moment and returned with a query of his own: "Are you married?" A little startled at the personal nature of the question, the woman hesitated before answering, "Yes, I am. Why do you ask?" The artist continued his line of questioning with, "And, do you have children?" Again, somewhat unsettled by the direction of the conversation, the woman answered hesitatingly, "Yes, I have three. Why?" The final question made the point, "And, which is your favorite?"

This short story illustrates the power of "discovered truth." In our culture, a question asked is most typically met with an answer to satisfy the question. We assume that the person asking the question is simply in search of the information that will satisfy their query. But is that really the best form of teaching? How much more powerful is the lesson when we refuse to give a simple answer to a simple question and instead, we aid the person questioning in the discovery of truth?

The artist in our example could have answered, "I have no favorites. I find something unique to love in each piece I create." However, the impact of that answer is not nearly as lasting or profound as the journey of allowing truth to be discovered in a personal and relatable way. Once the artist connected his emotional tie to each of his works with the emotional tie the young woman had with her children, she understood his answer in a way that she would never forget.

In the course of study you are about to experience, it is not our goal to issue answers to common questions. The course is designed to help you deepen your relationship with Jesus and become His disciple, and it is also designed to help you discover how to make disciples of those who desire to follow Him. However, it is not our goal to provide *information* and *processes* that develop a *program* for that purpose. It is our goal to help you discover the root of your relationship with God, and then allow you to guide others into a discovery of how they too can develop an individual love for the God—who created them and so desperately desires their affection. It is true that some portions of this study will be a bit more informational than inspirational. However, this information is always necessary to form a foundation from which we can understand the inspirational truth that transforms life eternally. This combination of information and inspiration has transformed everyone who has ever truly embraced the call to be a disciple of Jesus.

Discipleship is commonly defined as:

a. *One who embraces and assists in spreading the teachings of another.*

b. *An active adherent, as of a movement or philosophy.*

Biblically speaking, discipleship is not a casual encounter. Disciples are not periodic learners. As a matter of fact, discipleship may be one of the most misunderstood or misused terms commonly uttered in Christian circles today. It seems that little is commonly known about the meaning of the word or its use in the biblical text.

To begin, the word *disciple(s)* is found in 259 verses of Scripture (when reading from the NKJV translation). Of those 259 occurrences, only one is located outside the books of Matthew, Mark, Luke, John, and

Acts. That one instance is found in Isaiah 8:16. Since this is the first time the word is used in the biblical text, we can give it greater weight when defining the meaning of the word. The theological term for this additional weight is called "the principal of first mention." In legal terms, we would call this a "precedent" usage. That means that we must understand the context of what was happening at that time in which the word is used for us to understand the word.

That context is quite simple: The nation of Israel was about to be attacked by Assyria. God was speaking through the prophet Isaiah, forewarning His people that they would turn to sources other than Him for a solution to the Assyrian attack. Therefore, He instructed Isaiah to select a group of people to serve as guides and anchors amid the storms of war. He told Isaiah that in preparation for the upcoming response of the people of Israel, he should: "Bind up the testimony, Seal the law among my *disciples*" (Isa. 8:16, emphasis added).

The disciples of God were to guide the people of Israel through the challenges of circumstantial transition. They were to provide comfort in the face of danger and hope in the face of threat. The disciples of God were to counter the claims of those who said that the solution to their circumstantial problem was circumstantial response. God's disciples simply stood their ground and declared, "Should not a people seek their God? . . . To the law and to the testimony!" (Isa. 8:19b-20a).

Jesus's disciples followed this same whole-hearted commitment when they found others turning away (see John 6:66). In verse 67, Jesus asked them if they wanted to go away as well. Peter answered for the entire group when he said, "Lord, to whom shall we go? You have the words of eternal life" (v. 68). Discipleship is often countercultural, and always whole-hearted. Discipleship is the unwavering statement,

"I want to be like my Master." If we do not dare to become disciples, we have no hope of making disciples (see Matt. 28:19).

This course (delivered in two books: *Narrow Gate Notes on Identity* and *Narrow Gate Notes on Purpose*) is an invitation to change and deepen your experience with God by rooting yourself in Him. We will begin with the basic establishments of why we believe what we believe.

Throughout this study, we will learn to better understand our design as vessels of His love on earth, and we will couple that design with purpose. In the end, we will find a life of servant-hearted love toward those who are beginning the journey that we have been privileged to walk. As we learn to allow God to use us in the work of transforming other's lives, we ourselves will be transformed.

The journey will take us through four distinct areas of focus. *Narrow Gate Notes on Identity* will cover the first two while *Narrow Gate Notes on Purpose* will cover the final two. Collectively, these two books are designed to help you answer the two driving questions of the Narrow Gate Experience: "Who am I?" and "Why am I here?" The four areas of focus are:

- **Scripture:** Understanding why we believe that the Bible is the living, powerful, breath of God.
- **Sainthood:** Understanding the definition available for anyone who is "in Christ."
- **Sanctification:** Understanding how we move from infancy to maturity in our spiritual lives.
- **Servanthood:** Understanding the purpose of our Christian maturity.

As we begin, allow yourself to approach this process with a fresh outlook. Some of this material may be a review of what you already know; some of this material may be brand new. Please consider all of it with fresh eyes and an open heart. Allow the Spirit of God to teach you as you discover the truth of God's identity and purpose for all who call upon the name of the Lord and would dare to be a *disciple*.

CHAPTER 1

Scripture: Biblical Evidence

If we are to grow as a body of believers that can help one another through the transitions and challenges of life, we will need a guiding source of truth. If God is our guiding Source of truth, we must agree on whether the Bible is a valid source of His guidance, and a true expression of who He is. The discussion we are embarking on is designed to help us distinguish the Bible from other books. It is designed to expose us to truths that separate books written by individuals from the living document authored by God and recorded by His servants.

All Roads?

What is truth? That's the question Pilate asked of Jesus during the last hours of His life (John 18:38). The irony of the question lies in the fact that Pilate didn't stick around to get an answer. It's as if he didn't believe there was an answer to that question. Today, many would agree with that conclusion. More and more, we encounter a culture that believes *truth* is relative to the person experiencing it. In other words, you have your truth and I have mine. But if that is the case, then truth does not actually exist at all. Is it possible to establish truth as an absolute?

In early astronomy, it was thought that the observable celestial bodies orbited around the earth. When the understanding of earth's orbit around the sun was first proposed, it was met with social resistance. We can liken our understanding of truth to the discovery of how cosmological orbits actually work. Our early suppositions about orbit were based on people's egos, not fact. We assumed that we were the most important element of existence and therefore, logic would dictate that the universe would revolve around us.

In similar fashion, we approach philosophy with that same egocentricity. We adopt an attitude that says, "My experience is the best discerner of truth." We never stop to consider that truth may not be the relevant variable in the equation. We never ponder the thought that truth might be a constant and our experience with that constant truth is the variable. If that thought proves to be accurate, then the truth is no longer relative to the person experiencing it; rather, the person is relative to the truth.

So, what is truth? Don't all religions contain truth? Aren't all religions simply different paths to the same truth?

- Hindus believe that there are thousands of gods.
- Orthodox Jews believe that there is only God, and they are waiting for their messiah. They believe that Jesus was a heretic because He said that He was the Son of God.
- Buddhists believe that there is no god at all.
- Mormons believe that Jesus is the half-brother of Satan.
- Christians believe that Jesus is God.

Can these opinions be called paths to the same truth?

- Muslims believe that a man is judged in a balance of his good and bad deeds on earth.

- Hindus believe that man is not judged at all, but rather is reformed after each life in accordance with the enlightenment attained in the life that is expiring.
- Christians believe that people are judged according to their response to Jesus and His offer to be their Lord and Savior.

Can these opinions all be concurrently true?

The point is simple: Not all religions can be true because they blatantly contradict one another. Therefore, we must begin our journey by establishing what we will use as a source of truth. Buddha never claimed to be the truth. Mohammed never claimed to be the truth. As a matter of fact, no leader of a prevailing world religion ever claimed to *be* the *truth* (except One). They claimed to *know* the truth. They claimed to be enlightened according to the truth. They claimed to be prophets of the truth.

However, Jesus said plainly, "I am the way, the truth, and the life. No one comes to the Father except through Me" (John 14:6). He did not believe (or teach) that all religions were varying paths up the same mountain of truth. He stated clearly that He is the truth. Additionally, Jesus prayed, "Sanctify them by Your truth. Your word is truth" (John 17:17). When we couple these two statements together with the opening words of the Gospel of John, claiming that Jesus is the Word of God—and in fact *is* God—we find this conclusion: The truth is found in the life of Jesus and the Holy Bible. We must include the Bible in this scenario because Jesus told the pharisees, "You search the Scriptures, for in them you think that you have eternal life, and these are they which testify of me" (John 5:39). And since we have already established that these claims run counter to other world religions, we cannot hold to

the philosophy that all religions are truth. We must choose to accept or deny Jesus's claim to be the Truth!

To the Test

With this introduction in hand, we are forced to investigate the claims of Jesus to see if we can rest confidently on the fact that the Word of God, the Bible, is truth. We must ask whether there are proofs that we can rely on to add validity to the claim of biblical truth that we are testing.

To accomplish this goal, we will look at:

- **Biblical Composition:** How did we get the Bible we have today, and can we believe that it is accurate?
- **Patterns Within the Text:** Are there things within the text that cannot be accredited to the work of man?
- **Prophecy:** Does the Bible predict with specificity and then deliver with accuracy?

It stands to reason that if the Bible is the truth of God, then we should be able to find proof of that truth. If God authored the Biblical text, then it cannot be *like* other religious books. There must be things about the Bible that make it distinctly different from the Bhagavad Gita of the Hindus or the Quran of the Muslims. Is the Bible different?

What Is the Bible?

It has been said that there is no better commentary on the Bible than the Bible. So, we must ask what the Bible has to say about itself. For instance: Hebrews 4:12 says, "For the word of God *is* living and powerful, and sharper than any two-edged sword, piercing even to the division of soul and spirit, and of joints and marrow, and is a discerner of

the thoughts and intents of the heart." Second Timothy 3:16 tells us: "All Scripture is God-breathed and is useful for teaching, rebuking, correcting and training in righteousness" (NIV). Second Timothy 3:15 tells us that the Scriptures can make us "wise for salvation through faith which is in Christ Jesus." And Jesus told the Pharisees to "search the Scriptures, for in them you think you have eternal life; and these are they which testify of Me" (John 5:39).

These four verses alone tell us that the Bible is the living breath of God that is able to make us wise for salvation because they are written about Jesus—through whom we are saved by faith. That is a claim that no other holy book comes close to making. No other holy book says that it is the very breath of God. No other holy man says that the holy book is written about him. Only Jesus has the audacity to claim that the entire Bible is the living breath of God that testifies about Himself. Once more, we find that not all holy sources are paths to the same truth.

Remembering that Paul declared that all Scripture is inspired by God, we must ask if the text of the Old Testament affirms that claim. A quick search using e-Sword Bible study software to look through the NKJV translation will provide some startling answers to that question. Consider these phrases that appear in that search:

"Thus says the LORD" (418 times)
"God said" (46 times)
"God says" (8 times)
"The LORD said" (232 times)
"The LORD says" (6 times)
"The LORD spoke" (133 times)
"The LORD speaks" (5 times)
"God spoke" (12 times)
"The word of the LORD came to" (102 times)

That's a grand total of 962 occurrences where Scripture tells us that God is speaking. If the Bible is what it claims to be, there must be evidence to that claim contained in its contents. So, what are the "contents" of Scripture? Let's begin our journey there.

The Bible is a collection of writings that are represented in what are commonly called "books" of the Bible. These books include historical writings, poetry and philosophy, law, prophecy, and letters to individuals or groups. There are sixty-six books in total, and they were written by over forty different writers. We don't know the exact number of writers because some of the books were not penned with a writer's name attached. These forty-plus writers lived over a period of approximately 1,500 years.

Immediately we find our first source for testing the validity of our claim that the Bible is the breath of God. If this holy book was written by more than forty men in a period that stretched over 1,500 years, there should be some sense of contradiction to the writing. However, if God is the Author, and the writers were simply scribes who were dictating as they were led by the Spirit of God, then there should be no contradiction in the text because the text had one perfect Author. As we move through our study together, we'll find that this latter assumption proves to be true.

We will not assume that a few pages in a discipleship curriculum will settle the issue of inspired authorship with finality. Many books have been written for that purpose. If we truly desire to find a settling point in our hearts regarding the divine inspiration of the Bible, we can turn to authors like Lee Strobel and others who have spent years developing resources for just that purpose. For now, the intention of the information in the pages ahead is to introduce a brief synopsis that can speak to this claim of God's control regarding the Bible.

For instance, prophecy and miracles are two sources of supernatural control that the Bible records. In fact, J.B. Payne's *Encyclopedia of Biblical Prophecy* claims that twenty-seven percent of the biblical text is prophecy. If you remove the prophecy from the biblical text, the Bible ceases to be the Bible. It becomes a disjointed and incoherent collection of writings that seem to have little or no relation to one another. Unlike other holy books, the existence of the Bible is dependent on the issuing and fulfilling of its prophecy. Without prophecy, we cannot know that Jesus is who He claims to be. While that may sound like a bold statement, it is a merciful statement. God left no room for question in His announcement of the Messiah. We'll cover that issue later in this section, but for now we must realize that prophecy in the Bible is unlike any other prophetic collection because of its volume, breadth, and accuracy.

Additionally, the core tenets of Judeo-Christian faith are rooted in miraculous encounters. Jews received their freedom from slavery, their governing law, and the inheritance of their land through miraculous intervention. Without miracles, Judaism doesn't exist. Additionally, Jesus's birth and resurrection are two miraculous cornerstones of the Christian faith. If Jesus is not supernaturally born and raised from the dead, then He cannot be who He claims to be. Therefore, Christianity falters and disappears on the argument of miracles.

In contrast to this fact, all other holy books can easily have their prophecy and miracles removed with very little effect on the existence of the text. Remove the prophecy from the Quran and you still have the Quran. No book in existence is as dependent on outside control as the Bible. And the reason is simple: the Bible is claiming to be something other than a mere book. If it can stand without supernatural dependence, then it must be nothing more than the contrivance of man.

In the sections that follow, we will discuss some of the material that is commonly used to offer credence to the claim that Scripture is the living breath of God Himself. Again, our hope is not that we will offer an exhaustive discussion of the subject. Rather, we hope to discover enough evidence to put to rest any doubts that exist regarding whether God is the Creator and Sustainer of the Holy Scriptures.

Indestructible

If the Bible is a mere work of man, then men should be able to rid society of its existence. In fact, many men have sought to do just that. Here's a short list of attacks on Scripture for our review:

- Antiochus IV Epiphanes (215-164 BC) sought to destroy the Jewish laws and sacrifices by sacrificing a pig in the Temple of God and burning every copy of the Tanakh (Hebrew Bible) that his army could find.
- Emperor Diocletian (242-312 AD) ordered death for any person who owned a copy of the Scriptures. He allegedly said, "I have completely exterminated the Christian writings from the face of the earth." But when Constantine came to the throne and desired a copy of the Scriptures, within twenty-four hours fifty copies of God's Word were offered to him.
- Voltaire boldly declared that within 100 years of his life on earth the Bible would be no more. But the very press upon which he printed his propaganda material would be used later to print Bibles.
- Robert Ingersoll, famous American atheist of the 17th and 18th centuries, made the same outrageous claim: "Within 15 years I'll have the Bible lodged in a morgue." But Ingersoll is dead, and the Bible is alive and well.

- More than 100 years ago, creator of the former Soviet Union, Vladimir Ilyich Lenin, sought to remove every vestige of religion from Eastern Europe.
- Following in the steps of Lenin, Joseph Stalin and his cronies swept through every town and village to remove Bibles from his newly established "utopian society." Lenin and Stalin lie in their tombs, but the Word of God now exists richly in that part of the world.

This evidence is sufficient to make the argument that although many men have sought to rid the world of God's Word, man's attempts have failed, and God has prevailed. Despite these repeated attempts to silence the voice of God through His written Word, the Bible lives on in abundance to this day.

So, What Is the Bible?

The Bible has one central message; one central theme that runs throughout the entire book. The message is about a person. While many may think that the Bible is a series of "rules for living," but that's not the whole truth. As a matter of fact, that's not even the majority truth. The Bible is about Jesus, and the Book reveals Him as the Messiah who came to redeem and save mankind. Jesus is on every page and in every passage of the Bible, whether it be the Old or New Testament.

The Old Testament was finalized some 400 years before the birth of Jesus. The New Testament was written during and after Jesus walked the earth. However, these two parts are interconnected and have the same principles and topics contained within them. For every New Testament principle we discover, we will find an Old Testament record that paints a picture of that principle. As one Bible teacher, Chuck

Missler, says, "The New Testament is in the Old Testament concealed, and the Old Testament is in the New Testament revealed." The Old Testament is Jesus—the coming Messiah—concealed, and the New Testament is Jesus revealed as Savior of the world.

God has created the text of Scripture to invite us on a journey that has a guaranteed outcome. Deuteronomy 4:29 tells us, "But from there you will seek the LORD your God, and you will find *Him* if you seek Him with all your heart and with all your soul." God desires a relationship with us and guarantees that we will discover Him in that relationship if we put our whole heart and soul into the search. Therefore, He has designed Scripture in a way that invites us to invest ourselves in the journey of discovery. God doesn't give every answer to our questions quickly or easily. If He did, we wouldn't need to rely on Him. God wants us to seek Him, trust Him, and experience Him. Scripture even tells us that it is God's glory to conceal a matter, but it is the glory of kings to seek out a matter (Prov. 25:2).

Biblical Prophecy

We'll begin our review of Biblical prophecy in the book of Ezekiel, chapter 26, focusing on the city of Tyre. The modern city of Tyre is in present-day Lebanon. Ancient Tyre was a flourishing seaport city lined with palm trees and beaches. It is discussed in some detail in verses 3-5,7,12,14, where we read, "Therefore thus says the LORD God: 'Behold, I *am* against you, O Tyre, and will cause many nations to come up against you, as the sea causes its waves to come up. And they shall destroy the walls of Tyre and break down her towers; I will also scrape her dust from her, and make her like the top of a rock. It shall be *a place for* spreading nets in the midst of the sea, for I have spoken,' says the LORD God; 'it

shall become plunder for the nations. . . . 'For thus says the LORD God: "Behold, I will bring against Tyre from the north Nebuchadnezzar king of Babylon, king of kings, with horses, with chariots, and with horsemen, and an army with many people. . . . They will plunder your riches and pillage your merchandise; they will break down your walls and destroy your pleasant houses; they will lay your stones, your timber, and your soil in the midst of the water. . . . I will make you like the top of a rock; you shall be *a place for* spreading nets, and you shall never be rebuilt, for I the LORD have spoken,' says the LORD God.'"

In 585 BC, King Nebuchadnezzar of Babylon sought to overtake Egypt, the powerhouse of the day. As a part of his battle strategy, he turned his eyes to the strategic port city of Tyre. He intended to conquer it quickly and gain military advantage through its occupation. However, the Tyranians resisted strongly, and for thirteen years, Nebuchadnezzar campaigned to overtake its walls. Finally, he successfully seized the city. Thus the portion of Biblical prophecy was fulfilled: "Behold, I will bring against Tyre from the north Nebuchadnezzar king of Babylon, king of kings, with horses, with chariots, and with horsemen, and an army with many people" (v. 7). Now keep in mind this was written in about 590 BC, which is five years before Nebuchadnezzar began his campaign against the city.

Unbeknownst to King Nebuchadnezzar, during the thirteen-year campaign, the citizens of Tyre had instituted a covert campaign to build a new city on an island about a half-mile out to sea. When Nebuchadnezzar finally breeched the city wall, he found the structures of the city intact but wholly unoccupied. The citizens had fled to their new dwelling place. In frustration, he simply left the city and went on about his campaign without mounting an attack on the new city of Tyre.

In 332 BC, 253 years later, another conqueror came to the island city now called Tyre. Alexander the Great was determined to conquer the entire world, and he saw great advantage in possessing control of the city. Alexander commissioned several nations that he had previously conquered to help him sack the city of Tyre, hence, the fulfillment of verse 3: "Behold, I *am* against you, O Tyre, and will cause many nations to come up against you, as the sea causes its waves to come up."

In order to defeat the island city, Alexander and his men began moving stones from the ruins of the old city of Tyre into the sea in order to create a causeway that stretched out to the new island city. Alexander and his men moved every trace of the old city into the sea and left the land, upon which it once stood, scraped bare. Hence the word of the Lord was fulfilled that said, "I will also scrape her dust from her, and make her like the top of a rock" (v. 4).

Alexander moved forward with his campaign to capture Tyre and in a seven-month siege, he was victorious. He was so enraged at the difficulty he encountered during the campaign that he destroyed half the city and sold its 30,000 remaining citizens into slavery. However, that was not the end of the city. Prior to the campaign waged by Alexander, the women and children of Tyre were sent to Carthage for refuge. After Alexander's reign, the former citizens of the city began to return and re-populate.

By 1290 AD, Tyre was once again a flourishing metropolis. It had expanded from the island across the causeway and back to the shorelines of Lebanon. During this time, the Crusaders waged war against the Muslims. The Crusaders sacked the city of Tyre and made her the capitol of their movement. Within a handful of years, the Islamic

soldiers returned in full force. They arrived at the city of Tyre and were so disturbed that the infidels had defiled their city that they decided to destroy the entire place stone by stone. The Muslims threw all the "stones, . . . timber, and . . . soil" (v. 12) into the sea, and Tyre once again became desolate.

Today, little remains in the region that once housed the great city of Tyre. However, fishermen regularly spread their nets out to dry on the shore where the once-bustling city stood. Today it is little more than a dry, flattop rock surface. The city has never been rebuilt to its former glory, although freshwater springs near the city produce thousands of gallons of water daily, making it an ideal place to live. Hence the third part of this amazing prophecy is fulfilled: "I will make you like the top of a rock; you shall be a *place for* spreading nets, and you shall never be rebuilt, for I the LORD have spoken" (v. 14). When God speaks in Scripture, His Word is sure; He does what He promises He will do in predictable detail!

A Second Prophecy

In the book of Daniel, chapter 5, we read about the fall of the Babylonian Empire. The prophet Daniel once served King Nebuchadnezzar as his prime minister. However, approximately twenty years after the death of Nebuchadnezzar, King Belshazzar sat on the throne. Daniel had been out of the governmental affairs of Babylon for two decades. During all his life and service, Daniel's allegiance to God had never wavered.

When the Medo-Persian army set up camp outside the city wall of Babylon during Belshazzar's reign, the king laughed and threw a party. According to Greek historian and philosopher Herodotus (Book 1, chapters 18–181), the city wall of Babylon was, in modern measurements,

320 feet tall at its tallest point, 85 feet thick, and 56 miles long. It had 250 guard towers built into its construction. The outer wall stood as much as 100 feet high and approximately 11.5 feet thick. There was a gap of 26 feet between the walls, and a diversionary canal that was dug to re-routed water from the Euphrates River, causing it to fill the void between the walls. Offshoots from this diversionary canal passed through the inner wall and became the fresh water supply for the city. Babylon boasted a twenty-year supply of goods within the walls and considered itself to be the impregnable city.

As the king partied, he requested that the golden articles be brought from the Temple that was sacked in the Babylonian overthrow of Jerusalem in 584 BC. As he drank wine from the golden chalice, a finger appeared and wrote His judgment on the wall. Daniel 5:6 records that "his hips were loosened" and "his knees knocked against each other." The word "hips" is more commonly translated "loins." Belshazzar summoned his wise men and magicians to interpret the writing on the wall, but they could not interpret the meaning of the words. He offered great wealth and power to anyone who could interpret what he was witnessing, but no one could. At this point in our story, Belshazzar's "Queen" entered the room and told him of the prophet Daniel, who had served Nebuchadnezzar. Belshazzar summoned Daniel and offered the same wealth and power if he would deliver the interpretation. Daniel had little need of the king's offering, but he agreed to interpret the message of God.

In Daniel 5:28, the prophet of God announced that Belshazzar's kingdom has been taken from him, and verses 30 and 31 record that Darius the Mede conquered Babylon that very night.

Much has been written about Darius the Mede and Cyrus the Persian, and much argument has been offered regarding which of the men overthrew the city of Babylon. If you read Daniel 6:28, you see that Daniel served them both. While I encourage you to investigate details for yourself, I can tell you that the overwhelming evidence points to this well-balanced resolution to the debate: All secular historians record Cyrus the Persian as the man who conquered the Babylonian empire. Even the major Persian cuneiforms (primary scripts from Old Persian) discovered in archeological digs record Cyrus as the conqueror of Babylon. Why then does the Bible record Darius the Mede as the first king of Babylon after its surrender? According to Xenophon (the Greek historian and philosopher), Darius or "Lord" is a title given to many rulers. We know of four kings who were all called Darius. This is similar to having multiple Caesars or multiple Pharaohs. Ptolemy and Seleucid did the same thing after the division of the Greek empire, and we have multiple Herods recorded in Jewish history as well. Even the Bible records the Ethiopian Eunuch as being a servant to Candace the Queen, but we know that Candace was simply a title meaning queen.

This particular Darius is Cyaxares who is the father of Cyrus' wife, Cyrus' father-in-law. When Cyrus invaded Babylon, he gave the seat of prominence to his father-in-law for the last two years of his life (he was 62 and in poor health at the time of the invasion), and after Darius' passing, Cyrus took the throne for himself. Cyrus led the attack and Cyrus overthrew the city. Cyrus was the rightful king once Belshazzar was overthrown. However, he deferred the title to his father-in-law until his passing.

So, how did Cyrus conquer this "impenetrable" city? Many historians have recorded the events that led to the Babylonian downfall. As

Belshazzar partied, Cyrus had been secretly digging a second diversionary canal alongside the Euphrates River. As the sun set, the canal was opened and water began to flow into the diversionary canal, which lowered the river's level. This new, lower level allowed a band of armed and highly trained soldiers to enter the river and pass beneath the walls of Babylon, re-emerging on the interior of the city. Because Belshazzar had ushered in allegiance to Marduk (a Chaldean god) in favor of Bel (the Chaldean god worshiped by Nebuchadnezzar), the people wished for the removal of Belshazzar as king. They welcomed the soldiers of Cyrus because they saw them as deliverers from a king they did not want to serve.

Once inside, the Medo-Persian soldiers made their way to the gate and took temporary control of its function. They lowered the gate and made easy access for a waiting army to invade. There was no escape from, nor little resistance to the attack. The true fighting forces of Babylon were off making war with their general (and Belshazzar's father) Nabonidus, and the city fell easily. All of this makes for an interesting history lesson, but it comes to light as astounding prophetic fulfillment when we look at Isaiah 44–45. Let's begin by looking at Isaiah 44:24 and read through Isaiah 45:3. In those verses Isaiah writes, "Thus says the Lord, your Redeemer, And He who formed you from the womb: 'I *am* the Lord, who makes all *things*, Who stretches out the heavens all alone, Who spreads abroad the earth by Myself; Who frustrates the signs of the babblers, And drives diviners mad; Who turns wise men backward, And makes their knowledge foolishness; Who confirms the word of His servant, And performs the counsel of His messengers; Who says to Jerusalem, "You shall be inhabited," To the cities of Judah, "You shall be built," And I will raise up her waste

places; Who says to the deep, "Be dry! And I will dry up your rivers"; Who says of Cyrus, "*He is* My shepherd, And he shall perform all My pleasure, Saying to Jerusalem, 'You shall be built,' And to the temple, 'Your foundation shall be laid.'"

"Thus says the LORD to His anointed, To Cyrus, whose right hand I have held—To subdue nations before him And loose the armor of kings, To open before him the double doors, So that the gates will not be shut: 'I will go before you And make the crooked places straight; I will break in pieces the gates of bronze And cut the bars of iron. I will give you the treasures of darkness And hidden riches of secret places, That you may know that I, the LORD, Who call *you* by your name, *Am* the God of Israel."

We can see from this cursory reading that Isaiah's description of the overthrow of Babylon by the great Persian General Cyrus was incredibly accurate. Even down to the fact that in 45:1, the Lord declares He will "loose the armor of kings." The actual word for armor is the same word translated in other places as "loins" or "hips." As a reminder, Daniel 5:6 told us that this is exactly what happened to Belshazzar when he saw the writing of God appear on his palace wall. Additionally, God declared that the rivers would be dried up and the doors would be unlocked.

What makes this Scripture so astounding is that this account of the fall of Babylonian to Cyrus was written *200 years in advance* of the actual events. Not only did Isaiah not know Cyrus, but Cyrus' grandfather was also not even born yet when these prophecies were written. Furthermore, Jerusalem was still over 100 years away from being carried away into captivity. Clearly this passage of Scripture was authored by someone who had knowledge of the rise and fall of kingdoms before they happened. Clearly this passage of Scripture (as well as all of Scripture) is authored by God.

The Proof Goes On

As we stated in the opening of this section, it is not our intention to build a comprehensive case for the validity of Scripture. We are simply introducing evidence that leaves little doubt about the veracity of the Bible's claim that it is the living breath of God. Beyond what we have already discussed, here are a few more items for consideration.

Isaiah 40:22 tells us: "*It is* He who sits above the circle of the Earth." Isaiah's ministry took place around 740-680 BC (approximately 2,700 years ago). At that point in time, Isaiah wrote that God sits above the "circle" of the Earth. There were no astronauts, no Hubble telescope, and no pictures from outer space that would tell Isaiah that the earth was round. This is simply God speaking through Isaiah to offer proof that we can find if we are willing to exercise the "glory of kings" (Prov. 25:2).

Job 26:7 says, "*He* hangs the Earth on nothing." Job is said to be one of the oldest, if not *the* oldest, book in the Bible. Again, in Job's time there was no information on space, no concept of zero gravity, and no way that Job could have known that the Earth hangs on "nothing" but rather, floats through space.

No archeological discovery has ever conclusively disproven a biblically recorded fact. As a matter of fact, the opposite is true. Archeology repeatedly confirms Biblical accounts from the Red Sea crossing to the fall of the Jericho walls to the reality of David as King of Israel.

We have more manuscripts of Biblical text than any other ancient document. For instance, there are currently 5,686 Greek New Testament manuscripts in our possession. In comparison, the second most common ancient manuscript is Homer's *Iliad*, weighing in at 643 copies. This makes the reliability of the text beyond question.

Even the prophecies regarding Jesus give claim to the fact that the Word of God is a living document that declares the end from the beginning. Look at this handful of examples:

- He was to be of David's family (2 Sam. 7:12-16; Ps. 89:3-4, 110:1).
- He would be born of a virgin (Gen 3:15; Isa. 7:14).
- He would be born in Bethlehem (Mic. 5:2).
- He would escape to Egypt (Hos. 11:1).
- He would live in Galilee (Isa. 9:1-2).
- He would live in Nazareth (Isa. 11:1).
- His mission would include the Gentiles (Isa. 42:1-4).
- His ministry would be one of healing (Isa. 53:4).
- He would teach through parables (Isa. 6:9-10;Ps. 78:2).
- He would be disbelieved and rejected by rulers (Ps. 69:4; 118:22; Isa. 96:10).
- He would be betrayed for thirty pieces of silver (Zech. 11:1-13).
- They would cast lots for His clothes (Ps. 22:18).
- His side would be pierced (Zech. 12:10; Ps. 22:16).
- Not one bone of His body would be broken (Ps. 34:20).
- His dying words were foretold (Ps. 22:1; 31:5).
- He would rise from the grave on the third day (Gen. 22:4; Ps. 16:10-11).

Scripture even predicts that Jesus would make a triumphal entry into Jerusalem and does so with startling accuracy (Dan. 9:20-27). This prediction is particularly staggering because God told Daniel the coming of Messiah would happen 173,880 days "... from the going forth of the command to restore and rebuild Jerusalem" (v. 25). That command is also found in Nehemiah 2. Exactly 173,880 days from that decree is

the day we celebrate as Palm Sunday. On that day, our Messiah entered Jerusalem to the shouts of "Hosanna in the Highest!" That is a prophecy made 483 years before it was fulfilled! For a fuller understanding of how this prophecy times out in the Jewish calendar, I would invite you to read Nathan Jarrett's paper, "The Prophecy of Prophecies: Correcting Harold Hoehner's Interpretation of Daniel's 70 Weeks", located in Liberty University's online academic journal, *Eleutheria*.

And so, we return to our earlier claim that without Biblical prophecy, we cannot know that Jesus is who He claims to be. However, with Biblical prophecy, we can know with confident assurance that the man who claimed to be God is, in fact, God!

Summary

We began our journey of discovery with a question: What is truth? Our answer is clear: The Bible is truth. And it speaks of Jesus (John 5:39) who is the truth. It is unlike any book in existence because it is so much more than a mere book. Napoleon Bonaparte said of the Bible, "The gospel is not a book; it is a living being, with an action, a power, which invades everything that opposes its extension."[1] These words were spoken by a man who tried to do exactly that; oppose the Bible and destroy it. Additionally, Jesus is unlike any holy man because no leader of any lasting religion ever claimed to be God. They may have claimed to hear from God or have knowledge of God, but only Jesus declared Himself *to be* God incarnate.

Scripture is the living breath of God, and it is our tangible source of truth. It is the unfolding story of the lost humankind and a redeeming

1. https://bibleapologetics.org/did-napoleon-really-say-that/; https://biblehub.com/library/schaff/the_person_of_christ/napoleon_bonaparte.htm

Savior named Jesus. Throughout the entirety of this study series, we will use it as our guiding source. We do not find truth to be relative. Rather, we find our lives to be relative to the truth. The unique way each of us experiences the truths of the Bible is further evidence that God desires a unique, living relationship with each of us.

The text of Scripture will be our source for answers and guidance in our quest to become disciples of our Master and Lord, Jesus. May the Spirit of God give life to our understanding as we move forward in our journey.

Questions for Reflection

Thesis

1. The Bible is the living breath of God.
2. It is timeless and provably true.
3. It is verified by prophecy, historically accurate, and scientifically supported.

True or False

1. ____ My experience is the best discerner of truth.
2. ____ Truth is a constant and our experience with that constant truth is the variable.
3. ____ No leader of a prevailing world religion ever claimed to be "The Truth," except Jesus.
4. ____ Without prophecy, the Bible can stand on its own.
5. ____ There is one Author to the Bible.
6. ____ According to history, the Bible is indestructible.
7. ____ Job wrote that the earth is hung on a sacred thread.
8. ____ The Bible was written over a period of 1,100 years.

9. ____ Archeology has, from time to time, disproven historical facts recorded in the Bible.

10. ____ Nebuchadnezzar led the Assyrian army to overthrow Babylon as predicted in Isaiah 44.

Fill in the Blank

1. The Bible is the living ______________ of God (2 Tim. 3:16).
2. The New Testament is in the _____ ______________ concealed. The Old Testament is in the New Testament ______________.
3. The Bible is not a set of ______________ for living. Rather, it is a revelation of Jesus as the Messiah, who came to ______________ mankind.
4. Isaiah 40:22 tells us that the Bible declares the earth to be ______________ before scientists knew it to be true.
5. ______ % of the Biblical text is prophecy.

Short Answer

Explain the parallels between Ezekiel 26 and the history of Tyre.

In your own words, explain what sets Christianity apart from other religions.

CHAPTER 2

Sainthood: Man's Design

We are all on a journey—none of us have "arrived." When we take into consideration our shortcomings—as well as those of others—it allows us to extend grace and promote unity as we work together toward our journey of maturity. Understanding man's design will enable us to better discern between "cravings of the flesh" and "desires of the heart" (see Gal. 5:17; Ps. 37:4). Encouraging one-another by focusing on heart-issues instead of performance-issues will create an environment of collaboration, support, and fellowship that leads to true heart transformation.

In the pages that follow, we will discuss how man is designed to communicate for the purpose of developing relationships. Relationships are the vehicle through which love is expressed; love is the core ethic of God's existence (1 John 4:8-9). As we understand how we were originally designed to experience love and then compare that design with the predicament that man is born into after the Fall, we will find solid explanations for why we do the things we do. We will also discover the path to a restored relationship with God.

Understanding the nature of a restored relationship will begin to develop a hope for ourselves as well as those around us. That hope will

allow us to identify the successes and struggles in the sanctification process and aid those around us to follow the path to maturity in Christ.

Man's Design

In the previous section, we looked at Biblical design for the purpose of answering significant questions like:

- Is it logical to believe that the Biblical text is the product of man's design?
- Is there evidence that the Biblical text was authored by a source beyond man or nature?
- Does the Bible have a central theme or message?
- Is there an unchanging source of truth, and can we know that source and its intent?

In this discussion, we will look at human design to answer questions regarding the makeup and design of human existence according to Scripture. Since we have already established that the Bible is our valid source of truth, wisdom, and enlightenment, then we must defer to its opinion regarding our identity and God's intentions for our existence.

At different points in this section, we will use models to express ideas. It will be important to remember that all models break down at some point. Think of a photograph of a loved one and ask how effectively that photograph represents the individual. While we may agree that the photograph is useful, we would also agree that to fully know the individual, you would need to experience their presence. This holds true with teaching models, as well. While a photograph or a model may help us picture an individual, an idea, or even serve as an introduction, we only truly know them when we interact with them. The models that

follow are intended to be an introduction to a Biblical perspective of man's design as described by the Living Word of God.

The Model of Man

Genesis 1:26 says, "Then God said, 'Let us make man in Our image, according to Our likeness.'" Understanding what we can about the nature of God helps us understand the makeup and design of man. But let's be honest, we're not going to understand God. Therefore, we must accept that fully understanding man is going to be a difficult undertaking. There are mysteries associated with God that we'll have to accept as mysteries. Paul wrote to the church in Corinth, "Now I know in part, but then I shall know just as I also am known" (1 Cor. 13:12). There will come a day when our understanding of God, as well as our understanding of man, will be increased. But take note of the fact that this passage of Scripture is discussing the fact that for now we have a partial understanding that is limited by our habitation and corruption.

We know from Deuteronomy 6:4 that: "The LORD our God, the LORD is one!" This emphasis is replayed several times throughout Scripture, but it is no more well-known than in this passage. This creed helped to establish Judaism as the first Monotheistic (one-God) faith. However, we also see that God is Father, Son, and Spirit. This mystery of a singular God in three Persons is a separating hallmark of the Christian faith. The doctrine of the Trinity is an essential element in our faith. So, what do we learn from this truth of God's nature as it relates to man in His creation? Man is created in God's image, and this "three-in-one" pattern is found repeated in Scripture's discussion of our being.

A Brief Pause in the Conversation

Before we can move on, we must address a point of theology that can turn into a point of contention (if we allow it). For those who have never been introduced to the following terms, use this as an opportunity to expand your understanding. For those who are already familiar with the terms that follow, please approach this discussion with an open mind and heart to try and find some unifying truths between the two schools of thought.

For quite some time, there have been two commonly held theological viewpoints regarding the nature and constitutional makeup of man. They are most commonly called the dichotomous and trichotomous views of man. While there is no intention of trying to settle a debate in this short treatment of the topic, there is a desire to address the viewpoints for the purpose of showing that the two theological approaches are not mutually exclusive from one another. In the end, the hope remains that we can view these understandings of man's design as models that (in either case) break down due to our limited understanding of God and His creative abilities.

Theologians widely hold two common views of the constitutional makeup of man. There is a school of thought that contends that man is dichotomous or dipartite in his design. This school of thought contends that man is comprised of body and soul. This theological line of understanding also contends that soul and spirit are used interchangeably in the text of Scripture. The second school of thought contends that man is trichotomous or tripartite in his constitutional design. This approach contends that man is comprised of body, soul, and spirit. They find at least some form of distinction between the soul and spirit of man.

Again, the aim of this discussion is not to substantiate or disprove one of these theological viewpoints. Rather, our hope is to show that the commonality between the two is sufficient for man to understand some key points about his relationship with God. With our terms in place, let's dive into our quick Bible study.

Tri-di-choto-mou-WHAT?

Understanding theological jargon really isn't that hard. The truth is that theologians share a common language that has imbedded meaning so that they can have conversations that are pre-qualified. For instance: Golfers use terms like bogey, par, and birdie as jargon shortcuts that allow them to discuss the game in a pre-qualified fashion. Why write, "I took four strokes to get my ball in the cup, but the course only allowed for three on that particular hole," when I could just write, "I got a bogie on that hole." If we dig into the core of this trichotomy verses dichotomoy discussion, there are three Hebrew words that we need to know:

- *Ruach*: commonly translated as spirit or breath
- *Nephesh*: commonly translated as soul, spirit, or living being
- *Neshamah*: commonly translated as soul or spirit

Ruach first appears in Genesis 1:2: "And the Spirit (*ruach*) of God was hovering over the face of the waters."

Nephesh first appears in Genesis 1:21: "God created . . . every living thing (*nephesh*)." *Strong's Hebrew Dictionary* tells us that "living thing" means animals or breathing creatures. Additionally, this capacity of animal life is confirmed in Genesis 1:21,24, as well as Genesis 9:10,12,15-16. It is important to note that the overwhelming translation of this word is "soul."

Neshamah first appears in Genesis 2:7 in conjunction with the creation of man. It is from this verse that we will begin our look at the three words and their relation to one another. Genesis 2:7 reads, "And the LORD God formed man of the dust of the ground, and breathed (*naphach*) into his nostrils the breath (*neshamah*) of life; and man became a living being (*nephesh*)." The King James Version translates as "soul."

As we look at a couple of additional verses of Scripture, we find Elihu (Job's friend) speaking of God's creative and sustaining power in Job 33:4, where he states, "The Spirit (*ruach*) of God has made me, And the breath (*neshamah*) of the Almighty gives me life." In Psalm 33:6 we read, "By the word of the LORD the heavens were made, And all the host of them by the breath (*ruach*) of His mouth" (refer to John 1:1-14 to discover that this is Jesus). The purpose for including these verses in our discussion is to establish the fact that everything in creation exists by the will of God Almighty, the work of the Word of God, and the power of the Spirit of God.

Nevertheless, in Genesis 2:7 we see for the first time the Spirit of God being placed *into* creation rather than simply forming creation. In this verse, *neshamah* is forever linked to man. This word is never used in conjunction with any living thing other than man and God. Man and animals alike share a kindred use of the word *nephesh,* and that word is most commonly translated "soul." However, *neshamah* is reserved as a descriptor of man.

Before the panic button is pushed and anyone begins to believe that we are making the argument that man and animals exist in the same soulic relationship to the Creator, analyze what's being said. Yes, animals share some common capacities found within man: animals think; animals experience emotion; animals choose; they just cannot think,

feel and choose like we do. No, animals do not share in the *neshamah* of God and therefore cannot share in the relationship that man enjoys with God if he so chooses. There is a separating level of existence that comes from the fact that man is made in the image of God. That separating truth—that distinguishing factor—is the *neshamah* of God that was given to Adam at the moment of man's constitutional creation.

Look at what Solomon said regarding the spirit of man in Proverbs 20:27: "The spirit (*neshamah*) of a man is the lamp of the LORD, Searching all the inner depths of his heart." Solomon understood that there is a capacity within man that is not resident to animals or any other living creature. The echoed imprint of God resides within every man, so that all men may know Him. This distinguishing use of the word *neshamah* tells us that man has a capacity of the soul (*nephesh*) that is empowered by the fact that the Spirit (*ruach*) of God breathed our spiritual life (*neshamah*) into existence. Furthermore, this verse tells us that God utilizes that spirit as a mechanism by which He searches the inner depths of the heart. When the Holy Spirit of God calls to man's conscience, it is the *neshamah* that enables the heart to respond. This capacity for God inspired repentance simply does not exist in any "living thing" (*nephesh*) other than man.

If we view this unique nature of man and the inherent relationship found with the Creator in man's design, we find some unity between the dipartite and tripartite design within every human being. Whether we see the spirit as a separate component of man's constitutional makeup or a unique capacity of the soul of man that separates it from the soul of other living beings, we must agree that man has the ability to commune and communicate on a spiritual plane that is not available to other living beings. Whether dichotomous or trichotomous, the *nephesh* (soul)

of man has the ability to commune with God; at least that statement is true in the constitutional makeup of man. We'll discuss the loss of that ability in a moment but for now, let's resolve the fact that *neshamah* is simply not a capacity held within any living being other than man. While thought, will, and emotion may be present in many living things, the capacity to "commune with" or "be found in the image of" God is unique to man. Therefore, we can establish that a distinction between *nephesh* and *neshamah* are real.

We can also establish that *some* residual component of that *neshamah* is still with man, even in his sinful, separated state. The Proverbs 20:27 verse that was just discussed brings voracity to this claim. For additional evidence of this truth, we'll look at Isaiah 57:16, where God declares that if He did not relent in His contention and anger with man, "the spirit (*ruach*) would fail before Me, And the souls (*neshamah*) *which* I have made." Notice that the use of the word "spirit" is not capitalized in this verse. God is declaring that man has a soul with inherent spiritual capacity. The Spirit of God (*ruach*) created within man a soul which has spiritual capacity. This is how man communes with God in a way that no other living being is capable of doing.

The Two Shall Become One

When we began this sideline of thought, we established that the purpose was not to offer credence or criticism to either position (dichotomy or trichotomy). The unified truth of both positions is that man, as a living soul, *has the capacity to communicate bodily and spiritually.* Dichotomists would agree with that statement, and so would trichotomists. When man becomes mortally separated from those He loves, we refer to that state as mortality or death. In other words, man can

physically or bodily die. His soul does not cease to be. Rather, this state of being refers to the ability to physically commune and communicate with those who share a physical relationship, and you don't have to be a dichotomist or a trichotomist to agree with that statement. In the same way, dichotomists and trichotomists agree that God's promise to Adam in Genesis 2:17 was sure. In that passage, God says, "But of the tree of the knowledge of good and evil you shall not eat, for in the day you eat of it you shall surely die." Regardless of your theological school of thought, we all agree that Adam spiritually died on the day he sinned against God. His soul continued on, as is evidenced in Isaiah 57:16 (see the preceding paragraph), but he was incapable of spiritually communing with or communicating with God on his own volition.

Finding this middle ground of agreement between these two schools of thought, we can begin to draw models of understanding that will lead us to a discussion of how we were separated from God, the effect of that separation, the pathway to being rejoined to Him, and the effect of that redemption.

I will be using a trichotomous model to express these truths. I find it easier to express the truths of salvation and sanctification using this model. I am not purporting the trichotomous view of man as superior or inferior. I am not even suggesting that we should try and find some definite distinction between soul and spirit, as if they are two separated entities. Man is a contiguous whole and these models of division are only tools that allow us to approach a relationship with God in fuller understanding of our inherent capacities. I utilize this teaching model with a comfortable level of Biblical authority because even Hebrews 4:12 chooses to make a stated distinction between soul and spirit (*pneuma* and *psuche* in Greek). Therefore, I am proffering this model

as a mechanism by which we can discuss the rest of this series. Please do your own homework and make your own decisions regarding how you wish to picture these eternal truths. Always hold to the reality that models break down because we are limited in our understanding of God, His nature, His ability, and His plan. Always be grateful that God gave us His living Word and His Holy Spirit, so that we can know the truth of His love, even when we cannot define the details of His plan. *Thank You, Father, for going to such lengths to affirm Your sovereign love and grace toward us!*

Man: Three-In-One Composition

As our dialogue continues, please understand that all references to "man" are intended to be genderless. Announcing this evident truth will save time inserting parenthetic definition as we move along.

Body: Man has a body. Christian faith is not a prerequisite to agreeing with this obvious fact.

Soul: Beyond that, most everyone would agree that man has a soul (whether they know they would agree or not). The New Testament translates the Greek word *psuchos* (pronounced psoo-kuhs) as soul. We've already discussed the Hebrew use of the word *nephesh* as the most common word for "soul" in the Old Testament. We've looked at the ability to think, feel, and choose as a commonality between every living creature that is referred to as having a *nephesh*. Those three distinct abilities form what we typically refer to as a personality or psyche. The Greek word is reflected in this translation. Most people, regardless of religious belief, would agree that everyone has a personality. We'll have more to say about this

later but for now, let's list our last Biblical component of man's constitutional makeup.

Spirit: The spirit of man is a Biblical fact. We see the spirit of man introduced in Genesis 2:7: "And the LORD God formed man of the dust of the ground and breathed into his nostrils the breath of life; and man became a living being." As we have already discussed at length, the Spirit of God that was breathed into man distinguished man from all other "living things," which are linked to *nephesh* or soul. While soul and spirit both have etymological ties to the process of breath and life, we can easily rationalize that there is a distinguishable difference in the two because Hebrews 4:12 tells us that the Word of God is able to divide soul and spirit, and the Hebrew word *neshamah* is never used in reference to any creature other than man.

I have found that most individuals who claim the Christian faith have a ready understanding of body but great difficulty distinguishing between soul (*nephesh*) and spirit (*neshamah*), and an even more difficult time expressing definitions for these words. For clarification, let's state again that our assumed model will consider the soul to be our personality, which is comprised of how you think, feel, and choose. Common words used to describe these functions are *mind* (thinking), *emotions* (feeling), and *will* (choosing). The thing that drives life into these "soulic functions" is your spirit or your source of life that was "breathed" into Adam at creation, and then passed on to you at your physical birth. That (Holy) Spiritual origin is the resident echo of God's image that allows us to recognize and experience God in a way that no other living being can.

Many of us may try to insert Scripture that refers to the "heart" at this point and ask questions about why this component is left out of our model. Please know that it has not been left out of our model; it is going to be described and discussed later on. For now, let's agree to work from our "three-in-one" model of man. I've included a visual to help establish a picture that we can work with:

Spirit	Soul (Mind, Will & Emotions)	Body

The Role of the Soul

Let's begin with a simple observation: No two souls are alike. No one thinks, feels, and chooses like you do. Our soul is the individuality of our existence. Understanding the unique nature of the soul and the way it expresses itself will help us understand God's design for relationship and love. To gain a better picture of the role of the soul in the human experience, we must travel back to the garden of Eden and ask a few questions.

In Genesis 2:17, God says, "But of the tree of the knowledge of good and evil you shall not eat, for in the day you eat of it you shall surely die." As we know from the account recorded in Genesis 3, Adam and Eve did eat of that tree. The question that stands before us is whether God made good on His promise. Did Adam and Eve die on the day they ate the fruit of the tree? The answer to that question is an undeniable yes! God doesn't lie (see Num. 23:19). The problem that many of us experience when we answer that question is that we do not see Adam and Eve *mortally* cease to be. They continue to "live," but they are expelled from the garden. The thing we need to discover is not whether they

died. Rather, we need to discover *in what way* they died. This is where our model becomes valuable.

Did Adam and Eve die physically on the day they were put out of the garden? Some people would answer yes, indicating that the "process" of death began that day. However, God did not say that they would "begin" to die on the day they ate the fruit. He said, ". . . *in the day you eat of it* you shall surely die" (Gen. 2:17, emphasis added). *Adam and Eve did not physically die on the day they ate the fruit of the tree of the knowledge of good and evil.*

Did Adam and Eve die "soulically" on the day they sinned? The answer is obvious in the fact that they did not lose their personalities. They did not become automatons, so we must conclude that they did not die soulically on that day.

Understanding that the death they experienced was neither a death of the body nor of the soul only leaves one alternative. Did Adam and Eve die *spiritually* on the day they sinned? The answer is yes. Adam and Eve had constant communion with God until the day they ate from the tree of the knowledge of good and evil. On that day, God expelled them from the garden, and they were no longer able to commune with God in unhindered fashion. To better understand this concept, let's return to our earlier model.

Man has the capacity to think, feel, and choose. We have referred to that capacity as the soul of man. As man operates in those functions, his personality (soul) manifests itself as "physical communication." For example, right now, I am choosing to convey thought to you by causing my fingers to press keys on my computer. The keystrokes are recorded digitally, and a document is created. That document is printed and passed out to you, and you are causing your eyes to move back and forth

across the page to understand the thoughts I am recording today. My soul is now communicating with your soul, but we are using our bodies to facilitate that communication. We can communicate physically, verbally, or nonverbally. Thoughts and emotions may be printed, sung, or expressed through art or physical touch. There are numerous ways that our souls cause our choices, emotions, and thoughts to be conveyed to one another, but all those ways involve our bodies to some degree.

Physical communication originated with Adam. He communicated with Eve and his surroundings in the garden in much the same way we do today. However, Adam was also designed to commune or communicate with God through a second vehicle of expression: The God-breathed spirit (*neshamah* or *pneuma*) within Adam allowed him to be connected directly to God, who is Spirit. You see, God the Father does not have a body. John 4:24 says it plainly: "God *is* Spirit, and those who worship Him must worship in spirit and truth." When Adam communed directly with God in the garden, he was spiritually connected to his Father. When Adam sinned in the garden, he was cut off from that communion with God; he became "dead" to God. His soul was no longer able to express itself through the vehicle of his spirit, and he became spiritually dead. As Paul says in Romans 6:23, "The wages of sin *is* death."

To better understand this idea, imagine we are having a conversation face to face. If I were to stop breathing, if my heart stopped beating, if my eyes closed and I fell over on the ground, you'd probably call 9-1-1 and declare that I had died. But let's look at the assessment a little more closely. Have I actually died? Has my soul ceased to be?

As we discussed in our conversation on Biblical Evidence, we have to defer to the opinion of Scripture rather than relying on purely human

rationale. Luke 16:19-31 tells the story of two men (Lazarus and "the rich man"). The "rich man" died and was carried to a place called "Hades," a place of torment, while Lazarus was carried by angels to a place of comfort, "Abraham's bosom" (vv. 22,23). A chasm or gulf separates them. There the three men (Abraham is included in the conversation) discuss their current circumstances, make observations of emotion, thought, and will (choice), and refer to life as they knew it on earth. They recognize one another and even refer to people still living on earth as they speak. All indications from this text are that these men are fully alive (soulically) and engaged with one another. However, the story begins by informing us that both Lazarus and the rich man "died." We must ask the question, "What died?" It's simple: They are physically dead, but their souls continue.

If my body ceased to function, I would have no vehicle with which to commune or communicate with you. My soul would not cease to be, it would simply cease to be able to communicate by using my body as the vehicle of communication. On the day that Adam and Eve sinned in the garden, they died "spiritually." They lost the ability to use their spirit as a vehicle for their souls to commune and communicate with God.

The Effects of Sin and Death

What effect does spiritual death have on an individual? To best answer *that* question, we must first ask, "What benefit does spiritual life have on an individual?" When man is fully alive to God (spiritually connected), he experiences the benefit of God's presence and character. The apostle John tells us that God *is* love (1 John 4:8). Love cannot exist outside of relationship. That's why the nature of God must be discovered in the Trinity. God is in a loving relationship with Himself. He chose

to do the most loving thing that love could do: He chose to create man in His image, so that man could experience the love and admiration that only God can provide. Man was originally designed to be loved, accepted, and esteemed by God, and to reciprocate God's love with worship and service of His Creator. Adam and God were in loving relationship with one another, and the spiritual connection between them met every need of Adam's soul. That is the benefit of being in right relationship with God.

This leads us back to the opening question of the last paragraph: What effect does spiritual death have on an individual? When Adam chose to act independently of God's design, Adam was separated from his source of love and acceptance. He no longer had the deepest need of his soul met by God, so he had to find another source to satisfy that need. Since Eve was also made in the image and likeness of God (see Gen. 2:22), she became Adam's new source and supply. The problem began!

Because we are all born in the lineage of Adam, we are born "like" him. Birth determines our nature (our likeness or identity). Turtles give birth to turtles. Birds give birth to birds. People give birth to people. It's that simple. Offspring are always born into the likeness of their parents. While the feather colors may change slightly from bird to bird, they are all born birds all the same.

Once Adam sinned, he became separated from God and, therefore, *different* from God. He became "sinful," and that sinfulness became his nature. When Eve and Adam began to have children, those children were born into the nature or likeness of their parents: sinful. They were born with a sinful nature. They didn't become sinners because they sinned; they sinned because they were born into a nature of sin. It's just

that simple. This is why Jesus told Nicodemus that we must be born again (John 3:3-6): "That which is born of the flesh is flesh, and that which is born of the Spirit is spirit" (v. 6). We are born in the likeness and nature of Adam: spiritually separated from God and meeting our soulic needs through worldly techniques and sources. That is the process that the text refers to as "walk according to the flesh" (Rom. 8:4; see also 2 Pet. 2; 2 Cor. 10; Phil. 3). Jesus looks at Nicodemus and, in a sense, declares a simple truth: "You've been born according to sin, and you must be born again according to the Spirit. You need your nature changed!" We, being sinful by birth, have no choice but to look to one another for the fulfillment of our soulic needs. That statement is true until the day we are introduced to Jesus!

Adding to the Model

We have established the fact that the Bible is our source of truth. We have established:

- Scripture is God's plan to restore man into relationship with Himself through Jesus Christ.
- Our "three-in-one" existence is a reminder of the God who created us loves us.
- Adam's choice caused us to be born contrary to the design that God established in the beginning.
- Our soul expresses itself through our body in search of fulfilling its needs and we have called that process "flesh."

While the Bible does refer to "flesh" in terms of our material body (2 Cor. 4:11), it also uses the term to describe our soul's expression

toward and manipulation of this material world in its effort to find satiation (Rom. 7:5,18)

So, let's add to our previous model and see if we can create a more complete picture:

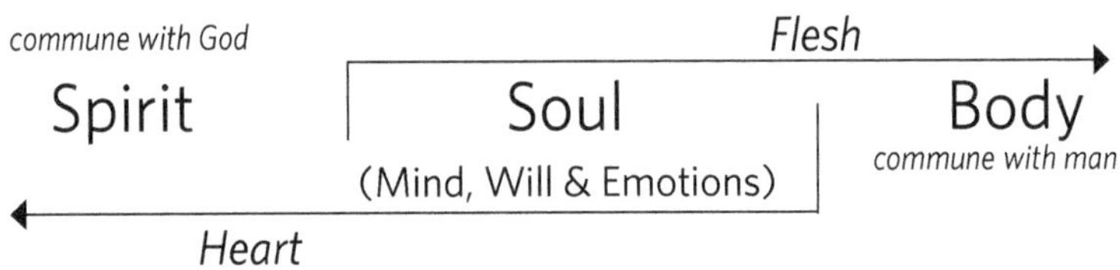

In this view of our model, we find two new words established: "flesh" and "heart." I have lost track of the number of times I've heard people quote the prophet Jeremiah: "The heart *is* deceitful above all *things*, And desperately wicked; Who can know it?" (Jer. 17:9).

I am not offering the idea that we should argue with Jeremiah (or God) in this assessment of man's condition. I am simply asking that we look at the context of the writing and understand that this statement is not a final indictment on man. Just look back four verses and you'll discover the context of the statement: "Thus says the LORD, 'Cursed *is* the man who trusts in man And makes flesh his strength, Whose heart departs from the LORD'" (v. 5). In verse 10, the prophet said that the futility is in trying to judge the heart because only God can do that.

The problem with the modern quoting of this verse is that it discounts *so* many verses of Scripture that speak of a regenerated heart. I'll only listed one here and will leave the rest for you to discover. In Ezekiel 11:19, God said, "Then I will give them one heart, and I will put a new spirit within them, and take the stony heart out of their flesh." Being born of the Spirit is the receiving of new life. New life comes with a new heart. It's not a sensation to be experienced as much as it is a fact to be

believed! God said it; that settles it. As believers in Jesus, we are new creations (2 Cor. 5:17). What once was dead (our spirit) has been born again (made alive). Our "dead-to-God" heart has been replaced with an "alive-to-God" heart. This means that *the ability to have our soul's need for love, acceptance, esteem, and hope can be met by our Father in heaven.* We can give up our techniques for managing and manipulating this world for the purpose of feeding our souls a diet that cannot sustain life.

Finally, we need to discover the ultimate benefit of this transformation. Since we can commune and communicate with God and man alike, we now become a conduit for God's voice to those who have not heard it. We are no longer hopeless and futile in our thoughts and speech. According to 2 Corinthians 4:6-7, we hold the "light of the knowledge of the glory of God . . . in earthen vessels." We have become vessels of hope because we have become the body of Christ (1 Cor. 12:27). God is now able to work for us, with us, in us, and through us. Look at the completed model below and you'll see how this re-born nature and alive-to-God heart allows us to become a conduit of hope: the hope of life! The red line represents the living hope of God as it passes through us to those around us.

This picture causes a new appreciation for Jesus's understanding of the two greatest commandments when He said, "'You shall love the LORD your God with all your heart, with all your soul, and with all your mind.' This is *the* first and great commandment. And *the* second *is* like

it: 'You shall love your neighbor as yourself'" (Matt. 22:37-39). It also sheds new light on our station in life as a "holy priesthood" and a "royal priesthood" (1 Peter 2:5,9).

Review Statements:

- The Biblical text has a design that cannot be logically and mathematically accounted for without the acknowledgment of a single Author, who knew the entire story at the different time of each section's writing.
- The "three-in-one" echo held in man's design helps us see how and why we are made the way we are:
  - The Biblical model for man's design includes body, soul, and spirit (three-in-one).
  - The Biblical model for man's soul consists of the mind (the way man thinks), emotions (the way man feels), and the will (the way man chooses). Again, three-in-one.
    - By the way, the mind and the brain are *not* the same thing. Your brain is a piece of meat, and it will die when your physical body dies. Your mind goes beyond your brain.
- The Greek word for "soul" is "psuchos," and we get our word "psyche" from this word. A lay term for our psyche is "personality."
- "Spirit" first occurs (with reference to man) when God "breathes" life him (Gen. 2).
  - There are three creations in the Genesis account:
    - First creation: all physical matter (managing not creating)
    - Second creation: all animal life (the Hebrew word *nephesh* is used here to describe the soul of an animal.

Animals have a mind, will, and emotions, but they are also limited in comparison to mankind.)

- Third creation: man (The Hebrew word *neshamah* is used here, which is important because it tells us that the soul of man and the soul of animals are different.)

- The formed body of man was inspired (brought to life through the Spirit), and the choices man makes from that point forward (combined with thoughts and emotions) formed a unique soul within man.
- The soul lives on after the body ceases to function (Lazarus and the rich man, Luke 16:19-31).
- Death is simply a separated state. You can be spiritually or physically dead.
- Birth determines nature. Because Adam and Eve were spiritually dead at the time they conceived, their children were born in their nature (spiritually separated from God).
- Sinning is not what makes us sinners. We sin because we are born sinners.
- "Walking according to the flesh" or "flesh" is the process of utilizing our bodies to gratify our soul's need for love, esteem, and acceptance (Philippians 3)
- The condition of man's heart is determined by his spiritual health (alive to God or dead to God):
  - The Scripture in Jeremiah often quoted about the heart being deceitfully wicked is talking about a person *who is trusting in idols or man or his flesh . . . not a Messiah* (Jer. 17:9)
  - We are dead in sin but alive in Christ (Rom. 6:11).

    - Ezekiel 11:19 establishes the fact that God renews our hearts by reviving His Spirit within us.
    - This is the process of spiritual re-birth that is described in John 3.
- Our re-born state (alive to God) allows us to simultaneously commune with God and man. We then become vehicles of God's love to those around us and are no longer dependent on man's esteem and acceptance for the sustaining of our souls. We get to live in the flow of love that God expresses for all men, and we derive our life and wholeness from that flow.
- Understanding all this information comes with the danger of knowing God intellectually rather than experientially. Becoming a vessel of God's love for a hurting and dying world is the key to living the life of "Christ in me" that God intends for all who are saved.
- Galatians 5:17 and Romans 7:18-26 depict the battle of "flesh" and "spirit."

Summary

As we bring this section to a close, it is paramount that we find confidence in our faith. I know that many of us would agree with everything that's been discussed. However, we may fall victim to agreeing intellectually and not experientially. If you do not truly believe your soul is eternal, that your spirit has been re-born and that your heart has been made new, then you will never begin to walk in the confidence that the newness of life can bring.

You will continue to operate in the paradigm of worldly thought, using fleshly techniques to try to provide what only God can supply—ultimate

benefit of this is transformation. Since we can commune and communicate with God and man alike, we now become a conduit for God's voice to those we interact with. And, to close with a Narrow Gate axiom, "We are best ministered *to* when we are ministered *through*."

Questions for Reflection

Thesis

God's three-in-one nature is reflected in His creation of man.

True or False

1. ____ Deuteronomy 6:4 says that God is one.
2. ____ Adam and Eve died soulicaly on the day they sinned.
3. ____ Man's spirit is the vehicle for his soul to communicate in the spiritual realm.
4. ____ Sinning makes us sinners.
5. ____ Being born again (John 3) allows us to commune and communicate with God.
6. ____ Birth determines nature.
7. ____ The body is the vehicle through which the soul communicates in the natural realm.
8. ____ All people are created in God's image.
9. ____ Man and animal have identical souls.
10. ____ The Spirit of God resides in no created being on earth other than humans.

Fill in the Blank

1. The soul is comprised of the ______________, the __________, and the __________________.
2. The soul's expression through the physical body without the connected Spirit of God is referred to as the ______________.
3. The soul's expression though the spirit is referred to as ________________ .
4. Adam and Eve died a __________________ death on the day they sinned.
5. Man cannot enter the kingdom of God unless he is born of ______________ and the ________________.

Short Answer

Explain how God's three in one nature is reflected in His creation of man.

Explain the difference between "walking according to the flesh" and "walking according to the Spirit."

CHAPTER 3

Sainthood: Who am I?

Understanding that spiritual growth is a process allows us to have mercy and patience during the life-long journey of sanctification. Seeing the progression play out in our own lives gives us the hope of change in others and allows us to empathetically serve while standing committed to the truth. If we anticipate change and growth and show mercy when it seems to be slow in coming, we'll have a better shot of avoiding relational drama, providing practical direction to others, and offering hope in the days when despair is the easier choice.

The key to actualizing the information in the pages ahead is in remembering a single truth: Identity controls behavior. We act in accordance with who we think we are. From the way we dress to the mannerisms of social interaction, we respond to the circumstances of life with an engrained personal identity. The question that looms on the heels of this truth is this: Who told you who you are?

If we are to properly serve the body of Christ, we must constantly call to mind the truth of who we are in Christ. Reminding ourselves enables us to empower those we serve. Succumbing to the accusatory voice of our enemy builds habits and attitudes that do not produce change. It is our charge to fend off the voice of our enemy by turning our face toward God in submission to His truth and will.

Identity: Who Am I?

In the previous section, we looked at the Biblical design of man and discovered some important truths, such as:

- God formed man with a body, soul, and spirit, and a man's soul is comprised of thought, will, and emotion. This "three-in-one" echo of God's existence reminds us of our Maker.
- We are born into the nature of our parents. Since our parents are born into a nature of sin, we likewise are born into a nature of sin.
- Biblically speaking, the word "flesh" is used to describe both physical existences, as well as the techniques we use to manipulate the physical world for the purpose of feeding the soul's need for love, esteem, and acceptance.
- The heart can be described as the soul expressing itself through the spirit. If our spirit is dead to God, then our heart is dead.
- The rebirth of our spirit causes the regeneration of our heart. Once we have an alive spirit, we have a heart that is alive.

As we move forward, we will discover how our reborn identity in Christ affects our daily life on earth. Many of us live in a constant sense of failing because we cannot seem to make our actions match our knowledge of the Truth. We read Scripture passages like 2 Corinthians 5:17 that tell us, "Therefore, if anyone *is* in Christ, *he is* a new creation; old things have passed away; behold, all things have become new," but we struggle to balance this verse with the experience of our daily actions, thoughts, and emotions. If this describes you, I have *great news*! You *can* live a life that is free from the guilt, shame, and dominance associated with sinful thoughts and actions. You *can* learn to face habits of life you

lived in your dead-to-God state (such as before your conversion) and overcome them by allowing the life of Jesus to live through you.

Understanding Identity

Ask children what they want to be when they grow up, and they will probably answer by telling you what career or social role they want to fulfill: "I want to be an astronaut" or "I want to be a mommy" are examples of this type of answer. Our society has created a paradigm in which even children learn to identify themselves by what they *do*. Even our names often work against us. For instance: My last name is Spencer. It is a British name that was given to an individual in a feudalistic society who oversaw the castle lord's provisions and dispense those goods as the community had need. So, this process earned him the title of "dispenser," which was later shortened to Spencer. Thus, my last name was intended to describe my position in the community. It formerly served to tell everyone who met me what I do. However, it has little to do with who I am. We used to live in a society that treasured a good family name. A household dispenser was a trusted man, so the name denoted trustworthiness. These days, family names have little to do with social standing. Instead, people's accomplishments and/or talents define them.

How shocked would we be to hear a young boy or girl declare, "When I grow up, I want to be courageous!" or "When I grow up, I want to be selfless and loving!" Children understand (usually better than adults) that the existential quality behind the desired social role is the real hope. Astronauts are adventurous and courageous. Mommies are selfless and loving. That's what children really want to "be" when they

grow up; they simply use the language of "do" to describe what they want to "be" because they learn that practice from us, the adults.

Who Told You?

In our conversation about man's design we discussed the fact that the words "personality" and "soul" are forever joined in the Greek word "psuchos." Our psyche is formed as information is gathered, choices are made, and emotions are developed. Since we are born into a state of separation from God, we must rely on the environmental influences around us to develop an understanding of who we are. Unfortunately, we do most of our learning (especially regarding personality development) in the first five years of life. Psychology tells us that by this point in life, at least eighty percent of our personality is formed and fixed. We learn our identity from parents, siblings, extended family, friends, enemies, bosses, subordinates—the list goes on and on. That means that we learn "who we are" from a broken source.

In contrast, when Adam and Eve walked in the garden, they were the beloved objects of God's affection. They were wholly identified by their relationship with their Creator. They knew no other defining source. When the serpent convinced Adam and Eve to violate God's command by eating the fruit of the tree of the knowledge of good and evil, everything changed. Genesis 3:5 states that their "eyes will be opened." Opened to what? Verse 7 tells us: "They knew that they *were* naked." They had a new view of self, coupled with a new vocabulary to identify them.

Let's not forget what the tree was called: "the tree of the *knowledge* of good *and* evil" (2:17, emphasis added). Up to this point in the Genesis account, Adam and Eve only possessed the *knowledge* of good. Do you

remember the account recorded in Luke 18, when the ruler came and called Jesus "Good Teacher" (v. 18)? Jesus answered deliberately, "Why do you call Me good? No one *is* good but One, *that is*, God" (v. 19). God *is* good! Adam and Eve had knowledge of good because they had a relationship with God. So, these questions remain unanswered: What does it really mean to have *knowledge* of good? What does it mean to have *knowledge* of God?

Knowledge is "to know." This seems evident. However, in Genesis 4, we find this word "know" or "knew" is used to describe the fact that Adam impregnated his wife (v. 1). The author uses the same Hebrew root word to describe "know", in the Biblical sense, as more than the simple acquisition of information. *To "know", in this usage, is to have intimate experience with another.* Adam and Eve had intimate experiences with God because He formed them, breathed life into them, and guided their lives. And, since God is good, it's pretty easy to see how we could say that Adam and Eve had a knowledge of good from the beginning of their existence.

Neither Adam nor Eve had ever intimately experienced evil until the day they decided to stand independent of God's command and pursue selfish desires. That choice—to intimately involve themselves with evil by joining their souls to a desire that was foreign to God's instructions—was the moment that their knowledge of good was joined with a knowledge of evil. Intimate experiences are used to define us! After Adam's act of rebellion, the awareness of his naked state was the defining characteristic of his existence. So, when God came looking for him in the garden and asked, "Where *are* you?" (v. 9), Adam answered, "I heard your voice in the garden, and I was afraid because I was naked; and I

hid myself" (v. 10). God's reply was simple: "*Who told you* that you were naked?" (v. 11, emphasis added).

Adam no longer accepted God's definition for his life. Because he had chosen to separate himself by becoming intimate with sin and evil, he now had to accept the definition that accompanied that decision: naked and afraid. He became defined by a brand-new relationship with evil. Adam and Eve *knew* good and evil. As we discussed in our conversation about man's design, God's promise of "death" in the day of sin comes true. Adam and Eve became spiritually dead to God. Their soul exists in a state of separation, and God is no longer their source of love, esteem, acceptance, and identity.

Reversing the Identification Process

Before we go further, let's do a quick recap. It's safe to re-state what's already been offered for consideration because this way of thinking is very linear and each segment of our journey toward discipleship will build on the foundation of understanding that we've already established. Reminding ourselves of the ideas that have already been considered will make this journey similar to climbing a ladder. Step by step we'll climb higher and higher toward an awareness that will transform us from the inside out—and isn't that the whole reason for reading books like this? So, here's a quick rehearsal of the rungs we've already discussed. When Adam and Eve were created, they derived their identity from the relationship they had with their Creator. They were loveable, cherished, acceptable, whole—the list goes on—because that is the way God dealt with them. Relationships and intimacy with God defined them, and they acted in accordance with that identity. Then a second voice entered their lives when the serpent told them a lie. They selfishly

chose to listen to the lie, and a new relationship was born. They became intimately acquainted with evil and, subsequently, became ashamed, afraid, and hid from God. These identifying words had never been a part of their existence before they chose to sin. God's promise of death on the day of disobedience became reality, and they were separated from the voice that called them beloved, cherished, and admirable. Now they were dependent upon other sources of definition that were selfish, independent, and cursed. Circumstance, environment, and people became the wells of definition from which they drew their water for life. No wonder the effect of sin was so devastating.

I like to picture this set of events by remembering when I was a kid, and my family would visit the state fair. One of my favorite things to do at the fair was to visit the side-show attraction that we called the funhouse. It was a series of mechanisms that allowed you to exist in an altered state of normality by shifting what you would typically recognize as normal into something slightly askew from what you expected. There were stairs to climb but those stairs would suddenly shift from side to side. There was a hallway made from a rotating cylinder that made your forward progress almost impossible as you tried to navigate the spinning floor below your feet. Jets of air would randomly spew up from the floor beneath your feet or the walls that you were trying to cling to for balance. The whole thing was disorienting and difficult and it made for a fun experience if you were a kid like me.

But the apex of the funhouse was the hall of mirrors. It was really more of a maze than a hall, and it made forward progress a confusing and frustrating series of laughs and screams. You never knew if the piece of glass you were staring into was a transparent barrier, or a free passage, or a reflection of yourself. It was always the last obstacle before

entering into the final room of mirrors, where everyone spent their last few minutes laughing at themselves and others. That final room contained a series of mirrors that were warped in different ways—whether vertically or horizontally. You would see a reflection of yourself, but it was never a true reflection. The mirror you stared into might produce an image of you with a tiny head and a giant belly. Or it might produce an image of you that appeared to be six inches wide and ten feet tall. But one thing was guaranteed: None of the images were actually what you looked like in real life. They were exaggerated and twisted replications that used some facet of your reality and then blew it completely out of proportion. The result in the funhouse was humorous. But, in some sense, we all suffer from the effect of that twisted reflection in our daily lives—and most of us never know it.

When we use anything other than the truth of God as the defining source of ourselves, we are effectively using a funhouse mirror to try and gauge who and how we truly are. The exaggerated or diminished state of the different facets of our being give us a distorted and inaccurate view of how we appear to God, to others, and to ourselves. When Adam made the declaration to God that he was naked, he was using the distorted mirror of Satan's accusation as the highest defining quality of his existence. He had always been naked. But now, that point of fact became a crucible of definition.

Unfortunately, the cursed and sin-influenced environment created by Adam's and Eve's disobedience is the reality into which each of us is born. Sin has its effect in (and on) our lives, and that effect manifests itself in our view of self and our view of the world in which we live. The real impact of this truth is felt when we realize the weight of the following statement: "Identity controls behavior." Nature gives way to

behavior, and behavior reaffirms nature. Here's a plain way of saying it: "Everything you do affirms who you think you are." Our view of self *drives* our choices and actions. If you doubt this truth, let me walk you through a quick exercise to prove the validity of what I'm saying.

Let's begin by having you pick a living member of your family or a close friend. Picture him or her in your mind. Now, let's suppose you go to sleep tonight as usual, but something strange happens while you rest. For some unexplainable reason, you wake up believing that you have now become the person you just pictured. I'll play along and add some commentary here to help the picture come to life. My wife's name is Stacy. Let's say that during the night, something happened that caused me to believe that I had become her. When I wake up in the morning, what will my morning routine be? Whose clothes will I wear? What car will I drive? Which cellphone will I carry? You see, everything I do will confirm my belief that I am Stacy.

This illustration is designed to allow you to see that you are not the sum of how you act and feel. As a matter of fact, the opposite is closer to the truth. The actions and emotions you experience each day are most typically a direct result of the identity you've adopted. So, now we're left with the obvious question: "How did you determine who you are?" What relationships and choices have you used to define yourself?

Adam began his existence with a definition derived from his relationship with his Creator. Adam's identity changed when he interacted with the serpent in the garden. You were born into relationships with the sinful nature and heritage that was passed from Adam. However, you too can have a change in relationship that is identity altering. That's what redemption is all about.

Before we move into a lengthier discussion about our redeemed identity as believers, consider with me the following observation. As we develop (especially in our first five years of life), we learn about ourselves by observing the reactions of the world in which we live in response to the choices and circumstances in which we find ourselves. We learn how to manage, mismanage, and manipulate the circumstances of life to acquire what we believe we need. In addition, we learn that there are limitations to what can and cannot be managed or manipulated, so we learn ways to avoid certain circumstances all together. At the end of the day, we learn to see ourselves through the eyes of the people we encounter regularly. Our identity takes shape as a *composite view* of what we think others believe about us. Never mind whether this picture is accurate; we genuinely believe that our opinion of their opinion about us is true, and we build an identity on that perception of truth.

The obvious flaws in this system are worth pointing out. First, other peoples' opinions are flawed because they are not valid sources of truth. Second, we can never accurately know what others *truly* think about us, so our opinion of their opinion about us is doubly flawed. We build a broken definition based on broken opinions that lead to a broken life. Thank God that redemption is available for anyone who wants it!

The Truth, the Whole Truth, and Nothing but the Truth, So Help Me God!

God is love. This phrase is easy for us to repeat because it's recorded repeatedly in the book of 1 John. However, the deep implication of this statement warrants a closer *glance* before we move on. I'll draw emphasis to the word "glance" in the last sentence because this is not intended to be an in-depth discussion about the previous statement.

Rather, I would like to introduce some simple phrases that can change your life, as well as your view of God, if you'll let them.

Love cannot exist outside of choice. Try to consider a scenario in which love can be forced. It's impossible! At the end of the day, love *must* be chosen. I must choose to love you, or you must choose to love me. We don't even have to mutually choose. It is possible (and common) for one individual to love another without that love being reciprocated. Romans 5:8 makes this painfully clear when it records, "But God demonstrates His own love toward us, in that while we were still sinners, Christ died for us." If God is love, then the ability to *choose* love must be inherent within God. But choice involves another variable, as well, so let's discover this next statement.

Love cannot exist outside of relationship. Any teaching that denies the doctrine of the Trinity denies this truth because love must have an object of its selfless choosing. God is the inherent source of all selfless choosing because He is in a perfect, loving relationship with Himself. We discover the importance of the doctrine of the Trinity when we accurately see God *choosing* to be selflessly sacrificial toward *Himself* (in three Persons). Relationships and choices: the cornerstones of love. Love by definition is "chosen (or decided upon) selflessness," and this love is undeniably demonstrated in the finished work of Jesus.

God, who is love, lovingly created man for the purpose of experiencing love. When man chose to become independent of his Creator, God lovingly allowed that choice to separate Himself from man. In Christ, God lovingly chose to remove the barrier and restore that relationship. We find this life-changing truth expressed in Colossians 2:14 and 2 Corinthians 5:21, in which God declares that He has nailed the righteous requirements of the Law to the cross by making Jesus, who

knew no sin, to become sin for us. As a result, in Jesus we may become the righteousness of God.

And there it is: The open pathway that revives the heart, gives new birth to the spirit, and redeems the soul. Our new identity exists because a new relationship of intimacy is available. We have been redeemed, and yet most Christians don't have a clue of how to employ this truth for effective life change!

If we are made in God's image, then we must accept that we are designed to love and to be loved. If we have been redeemed (or bought back) into relationship with God, then there must be a purpose for that relationship. We discussed this purpose in the last section of this book, but it bears repeating here. We have been bought back into a relationship, so that we might become the vessels of His love to a spiritually hurting and dying world. Remember the diagram that showed the reborn heart allowing God's love to pass through us? Remember 2 Corinthians 4:7, which says we are the earthly vessels that hold the light of the glory of the gospel of God as seen in Jesus? I am hidden in Christ so that He might be revealed in me. The verses of Scripture that describe "me in Him" and "Him in me" are the defining verses of our lives as believers. They are sacred text that God uses to tell us how *He* defines us.

And now, we must decide how we'll move forward in this journey of life. We can either continue to accept the broken, sin-influenced definition of self that is born from a disconnected and cursed world, or we can accept the life-giving, loving definition of the Father. The latter definition leads to purpose, wholeness, and the conquering of sin. The choice is ours. Sadly, most people who say they want to accept God's truth as the defining words of life don't even know what God says. At the close of this section, we'll look at a short list of what God says about anyone

who is "in Christ." In case you're wondering whether you are "in Christ," ask yourself where your trust lies regarding eternal salvation. Romans 6 clearly teaches that for those of us who have placed our trust in Jesus, we were in Him when He was crucified. We were in Him when He was buried. We were in Him when He was raised from the dead. And we are still in Him, seated at the right hand of God (Eph. 1:20; Col. 3:3). We *are* hidden in Christ, and we are *defined* in Christ.

Who Am I?

There are over 150 verses of Scripture in the New Testament that deal with the concept of "in Christ." Books have been written that fully cover the subject, so we won't repeat the process here. I only intend to pick a few verses and begin an exercise that will allow you to discover the depth and richness of this "in Christ" truth. As we step into this next segment of our journey, we must keep Hebrews 11:6 in mind, which says, "without faith *it is* impossible to please *Him* (God), for he who comes to God must believe that He is, and *that* He is the rewarder of those who diligently seek Him." Believing the truths that we are about to discuss is an absolute necessity in the process of seeing these things manifested in our lives.

One more caveat before we proceed: Truth is not generated from thought, will, or emotion. Truth is a facet of the character of God. If God declares something to be truth, it is! Jesus set the stage for this reality when He incorporated a teaching moment with His disciples in the upper room during their last Passover meal together. He told Thomas, "*I am* the way, *the truth* and the life" (John 14:6, emphasis added). Since Jesus is God, and since Jesus is the truth, what He says is final. It is not necessarily an emotion to be felt. Rather, it is a fact to be learned,

believed, and experienced. The process of believing God brings pleasure to Him, an ideology that is summed up in Romans 12:2: "Do not be conformed to this world, but be transformed by the renewing of your mind, that you may prove what *is* that good and acceptable and perfect will of God." The transformation process requires us to *know the truth;* and the truth we *know* (have intimate experience with) will make us free (John 8:32).

Second Corinthians 5:17 declares that we are not who we were! Remember that redemption and salvation affect the entire man—body, soul and spirit. However, 2 Corinthians 2 and Romans 8 (as well as many other passages of Scripture) clearly teach that the bodily redemption of man will come later. Second Corinthians 5:17 states that *all* things have become new. This is a statement of current reality and of promised truth. Second Corinthians 4:16, Ephesians 4:23, and Colossians 3:10 all draw a picture of the fact that our renewal is a continual process, and it is one that happens internally until the redemption of our bodies at the appearance of Jesus. Paul writes this truth in 2 Corinthians 5:17 because he knows the promise of God is sure. *All* things have been made new, but the reality of that truth is made manifest in our lives as a process. *The pace and sureness of that process is determined by how well we understand and implement the verses that describe the process.*

We'll take a deeper look at this transforming discipline as we continue our discussion in the next book, *Narrow Gate Notes on Purpose*. For now, we must start with an absolute statement: I am a new creation in Christ. I have been made new. I am born again (according to John 3 and Romans 6), and I am not who I was. My spirit is reborn; my mind is being renewed; my soul is being transformed; and my body is destined

for redemption. *I am new!* I am *not* condemned. Rather, I am free from the law of sin and death, and I am a beneficiary of the law of spirit and life (Rom. 8:1-2).

I cannot recall the number of occasions in which brothers and sisters in Christ have told me they lack confidence in their salvation. They typically express questions about their eternal security based on their life performance in comparison to their understanding of God's will for their lives. They allow their less-than-perfect behavior to become Satan's impetus for questioning God's ability to save them in their failing. The truth is that God has *already saved* us in our failing, He *is saving* us in our failing, and He *will continue to save* us in our failing—because He saves us according to *His* success. It's Jesus's performance (not ours) that buys us back into a relationship with God. However, if we live from a fearful position of disbelief, it will be impossible to live a life that is acceptable, pleasing, and complete in the eyes of the Father who rescued us.

"Now thanks *be* to God who always leads us in triumph in Christ, and through us diffuses the fragrance of His knowledge in every place" (2 Cor. 2:14). God will always lead us in triumph, and we can become the vessel that spreads God's fragrance among those who do not know Him. This is the type of "in Christ" verse that can change your existence, if you'll let it. If you made an unfaltering decision to accept this verse as truth and live every breath of your day today in harmony with this truth, how different would you appear to those around you? The question is: Why don't we?

Again, we'll discuss the implementation of this process in the next book as we begin to move from our identity in Christ to our purpose in this world. For now, I only want to point out the fact that God says we

are led in triumph. Therefore, we must stop declaring so much of our circumstantial existence as *failing*. If we truly believe that the definition of victory is left to God's design and vocabulary, then we must spend every day in the knowledge of the fact that God is leading us in victory and this march never pauses or ends.

"So we, *being* many, are one body in Christ, and individually members of one another" (Rom. 12:5). We are members of the same body and not just good friends on a spiritual journey together. Paul uses the way we care for our earthly bodies as a metaphor for the way we should care for one another. We have an obligation to one another that reaches far beyond fondness or social encounters. We literally belong to one another as much as our hands belong to our arms.

"Yet indeed I also count all things loss for the excellence of the knowledge of Christ Jesus my Lord, for whom I have suffered the loss of all things, and count them as rubbish, that I may gain Christ and be found in Him, not having my own righteousness, which *is* from the law, but that which *is* through faith in Christ, the righteousness which is from God by faith" (Phil. 3:8-9). We possess the righteousness of Jesus in the eyes of God. Remember our earlier discussion in which we said identity controls behavior? If we truly believe we have been given the righteousness of Jesus, how will we respond? If God declares us to be righteous, whose voice is telling us we are unworthy, unrighteous, failing, falling, sinful, and at risk of judgment? *Who told you that you are naked?* And who is telling you that you are clothed in Christ? You are not naked! You have been robed in the righteousness of Jesus Himself. You've never been more radiantly dressed in your entire existence. Start celebrating!

Final Thoughts

Most of us would agree that God's Word is truth. Most of us would agree that God's opinion on any subject is more enlightened and valuable than our own. We have established the fact that God is the living Author of the Living Word. We have effectively delivered the truth that through faith (trust), we have been spiritually reborn into the righteousness of Jesus and the power of the Spirit that raised Him from the dead.

Therefore, we are now obligated to believe what God says regarding Himself, His Son, His Spirit, and us. If God says we are "made holy," then it is true. If God says we are "led in triumph," then it's true. If God says we are no longer slaves to sin but rather sons of the Most High God, then it's true. So this question remains: "Why don't our actions line up with these truths?" The most concise answer is simply that we don't believe it. Most of us still view ourselves as sinful, unworthy, unrighteous, powerless, and ill-equipped for the task.

A quick lesson in Greek theater will help us here. All the actors on the stage of Greek theater were male. Two acting troops comprised the full cast of any play. The members of the first troop were called the "hectors," and they played all male roles in the production. They were men playing the parts of men, and we get our modern word "actor" from this Greek word "hector." The second troop of actors were called the "hypocrites." You can already tell what English word we derive from this original usage. The hypocrites were actors that played any part in the production other than a man: women, children, animals, gods, demagogues, plants, and everything else in the play were represented by men *pretending to be something other than what they were.*

In modern society, we tend to predetermine that all people are flawed and "human" by our definition. Therefore, any person who has

the influence of sin in their lives yet tries to live righteously by worshiping a forgiving God or talking about the truth of God to those they encounter immediately obtains the label of "hypocrite." This label is almost always applied as they carry out righteous behavior. A closer look at the true meaning of the word helps us understand that *we are only being hypocritical when we act contrary to the truth of who God says we are*. The feeling of hypocrisy that torments most of us in our efforts to act in accordance with God's declared truth of our identity is nothing more than that—a feeling! Feelings are *not* a valid source of truth. We need to wrestle against this concept that we need to be "true to our feelings" when that definition runs counter to what God says about us.

Hypocrisy ends when we become honest in our assessment of self. Hypocrisy ends when we finally stop quoting, "I'm just a sinner saved by grace" and begin stating emphatically, "I am a *saint* who still lives in a body influenced by sin."

God, hasten the day when we are finally delivered into our resurrected state and live in Your unfiltered glory! Until then, give us grace to overcome and hold fast to the truth that You have declared about us: We are Your beloved, adopted, engrafted, sealed, sanctified, servant children!

Here's a short list of the *truth* of who you are in Christ and the corresponding Scripture references:

- Romans 3:24: I am justified and redeemed (already).
- Romans 6:6: My old self was crucified.
- Romans 8:2: I am free from the Law of sin and death.
- Romans 15:7: I am accepted.
- 1 Corinthians 1:2: I am sanctified (holy, set apart).
- 1 Corinthians 1:30: I have wisdom, righteousness, sanctification, and redemption.

- 2 Corinthians 2:14: I am *always* led in His triumph.
- 2 Corinthians 3:14: My hardened mind has been removed.
- 2 Corinthians 5:17: I am a new creation.
- 2 Corinthians 5:21: I am the righteousness of God.
- Galatians 2:4: I am liberated.
- Ephesians 1:3: I am blessed with every spiritual blessing in heaven.
- Ephesians 1:4: I am chosen, holy, and blameless before God.
- Ephesians 1:7: I am redeemed, forgiven.
- Ephesians 1:10-11: I have obtained an inheritance.
- Ephesians 2:5: I am alive (formerly a dead spirit).
- Ephesians 2:6: I am seated in heaven (already).
- Ephesians 2:10: I am created for good performance.
- Ephesians 2:13: I have been brought near to God.
- Ephesians 3:12: I have boldness and confident access to God.
- Ephesians 5:8: I was formerly darkness but now am light.
- Ephesians 5:30: I am a member of His body (not inferior to other members).
- Philippians 4:19: I have all my needs (not greed) supplied.
- Colossians 2:10: I am raised up with Him.
- Colossians 3:3: My life is hidden with Christ in God.

Questions for Reflection

Thesis

Identity controls behavior and God declares us to be saints.

True or False

1. ____ People's accomplishments or talents define them.
2. ____ Love cannot exist outside of choice.
3. ____ How you feel is a valid source of truth.
4. ____ I am a saint.
5. ____ There are over 150 verses of Scripture that deal with the concept of "Christ in me."
6. ____ Birth determines nature.
7. ____ Adam and Eve knew both good and evil before they sinned.
8. ____ Our choices and actions are an affirmation of who we believe ourselves to be.
9. ____ Love can exist outside of relationship.
10. ____ To "know" (in the biblical sense) is to have an intimate experience with another.

Fill in the Blank

1. Eighty percent of our ______________ is formed by the age of five.
2. Because we are made in God's image, we are designed to ______________ and be ____________ .
3. Anyone who is ______ ____________ is a new creation.
4. Our view of ____________ drives our choices and actions.
5. We are no longer slaves to ____________, but rather children of the Most High God.

Short Answer

Before rebirth in Christ, what did you use to define yourself?

If we have been reborn in Christ, why don't our actions perfectly reflect this truth?

CHAPTER 4

Moving Forward

One of the people I love most in this world is a man that I've shared the privilege of ministering with for two decades. His name is Eric Davis but most everyone in the Narrow Gate Family calls him Boots. It's funny how quickly and innocently a nickname can be born, and I won't go into the details of how his came about. I'll only say that when someone from Milwaukee, Wisconsin, migrates to the south and brings their accent along for the journey, people notice. The way Eric said the word "boots" (especially when he was tired) was significantly different from the way most everyone else said the word.

But it wasn't Eric's dialect that made him a fast friend to most everyone he encountered. The thing that made (and still makes) Eric so immediately loveable to everyone he meets is his combination of humble character and quick sense of humor. He tells jokes that are funnier to him than anyone else—and then has no hesitation in laughing more quickly than anyone in earshot.

But his humorous and optimistic view on life also gives way to an authenticity of character that I've witnessed in very few people. Eric is an honest man. He takes the time to consider things fully before forming a position. He rarely accepts something as true or false simply because someone else claimed that it was so. He takes the time to

assess, consider, and balance a variety of factors before he settles into a position that he believes he can support with a clear conscience.

On more than one occasion, I've heard Eric sit and talk about the teachings found in the book of James. There are two points that he lands on with some significant weight, and I'd like to introduce them here before we look at a passage from that book and see how it might have its effect on our lives.

First, Eric is always quick to point out that James was written by Jesus's half-brother. Then, because he has a tendency to use humor as a vehicle to deliver very serious truth, he'll go on to talk about his own brothers. He regales listeners with stories of how he grew up with three brothers who regularly proved that mischief was the substance of young, male life. And when he has his listener settled with a good dose of laughter, he introduces the idea of how hard it would be to treat any of his brothers seriously if they claimed that they were actually God incarnate.

Then he'll return to the book of James and remind people that this author, James, grew up knowing Jesus as his older brother. James was not one of the Twelve chosen disciples who followed Jesus for three years of earthly ministry. He tells people that if anyone on earth had the right to discount Jesus's claim of deity, it would have been a brother who grew up believing that this "so-called-savior" was just a kid from Nazareth, who cried and bled and laughed and played like every other kid.

But that's not what James did. After Jesus's death, burial, and resurrection, James became such a believer in the claims of Jesus that—according to tradition—he was martyred by stoning through an order of the High Priest Ananus ben Ananus in 62 AD. So, when we read the text

of the book of James in the New Testament, we can feel fairly confident that he's writing with a level of conviction that few people have ever possessed.

Secondly, Eric is quick to point out that James is not most effectively read if we view it as a book of pure instruction. Rather, James is a book of wisdom. It dovetails perfectly with Jesus's teachings in Matthew 5–7, that we commonly refer to as the Sermon on the Mount. And, since Jesus was not trying to establish a new set of behavioral standards for self-righteousness by telling us to pluck out our eyes or chop off our hands (see Matt. 5:29-30), we should not believe that James is creating a new standard of righteous behavior for the believer to use as a measuring stick of works-based-worth.

Let me say it again: James is a book of wisdom. It's a great framework for us to consider as an ideal approach to how we think and live. But it cannot be implemented as a measuring stick that we allow Satan to use to attack our worth in the sight of God. When we fail to perform the way that James prescribes, it should build gratitude for the mercy of God that saves us in spite of our shortcomings, not condemnation for the fact that we cannot live perfectly sinless lives. Sanctification is an iterative journey that sets the horizon as our goal and then compels us to move toward it. The horizon is always within sight but never truly attainable because every time you move, the horizon moves with you.

Christian maturity is not a destination any more than mortal maturity. It's a process that seeks to take stock of where we are today and envision where we would like to be somewhere down the road. Likewise, sanctification is not a standard that is designed to breed guilt and doubt about our salvation or our worth. Rather, sanctification is the experience of renewing our commitment to allow the life of Jesus to be more

and more the reality of our daily journey through this world. Yes, we are already spiritually sanctified in the sight of God. We've already been made perfect (complete) "in Christ." But the process of earthly sanctification is a sojourn that allows Jesus's life to become more and more evident in our daily experience.

Stated simply, we are already hidden in Christ with God, which means that our eternal salvation is no longer in question. "For you died, and your life is hidden in Christ with God" (Col. 3:3). Hebrews says it this way, "For by one offering He has perfected forever those who are being sanctified" (Heb. 10:14). And here's why that second Scripture reference *really* matters in this discussion. As we begin to talk about how we move forward, it is important to understand that we cannot see our imperfect attempts at sanctified behavior as a disappointment to God. You are perfected forever in the sight of God, while you are simultaneously *being* sanctified in your journey through this world.

Think of it this way: If you had a son or daughter who was just learning to walk, how disappointed would you be when they took their first step and then fell immediately down on their diaper? You wouldn't be disappointed at all. You would shout for joy when you witnessed that first step! It's a seminal moment in the life of a child. It's a sign that he or she is no longer content to crawl on all fours and depend on their parent to be carried to wherever their heart desires to be. But it is no guarantee that the road ahead is going to be free of falls and injuries. The opposite is true. The question is not whether that child will fall but how quickly he or she will get back up and try again. Every fall comes with an opportunity to learn. Every injury gives birth to a painful memory that serves as a warning for future attempts. But no child ever capitulates to the difficulty of the task just because it's difficult. And neither can we.

Our spiritual walk begins with one big first step that everyone can and should celebrate. But don't mistake that celebration for a declaration that we have somehow mastered the art of walking. The steps ahead come with a guarantee that we are all destined to fall and get injured as we learn how to walk, skip, run, and dance our way through spiritual life. So, when the missteps happen, it's necessary to remember that our Father is not in heaven chastising us for our inability to immediately master the difficulties of sanctified life.

We were born into a world of sin, and we are constantly haunted by the memory of who we were before Jesus rescued us from our plight. Paul goes into great detail about this struggle between flesh and mind in Romans 7. I'd suggest we all rehearse it again and again to remind ourselves of the fact that much of the New Testament is filled with instructions that are given as benchmarks or guideposts along the journey of sanctification. But they are almost always offered after a discussion about how the saving grace of God has guaranteed our place with Him in heaven and our unchangeable identity in Christ.

With that understanding on the table, let's look at a passage from the book of James and then see how we can employ the wisdom it offers to move closer to the goal of "Christ-in-me" and "me-in-Christ" that we all hope for. Here's what James says, "Therefor, lay aside all filthiness and overflow of wickedness, and receive with meekness the implanted word, which is able to save your souls. But be doers of the word, and not hearers only, deceiving yourselves. For if anyone is a hearer of the word and not a doer, he is like a man observing his natural face in a mirror; for he observes himself, goes away, and immediately forgets what kind of man he was. But he who looks into the perfect law of liberty and

continues *in it*, and is not a forgetful hearer but a doer of the work, this one will be blessed in what he does" (Jas. 1:21-25).

The law of liberty that James refers to is the cure for the law of sin and death that once ruled our lives. Look at how Paul phrases it in his letter to the church in Rome: "For the law of the Spirit of life in Christ Jesus has made me free from the law of sin and death" (Rom. 8:2). But James offers his words in a tone that seems to be very boolean. It's as if he's declaring that we are either this or that, good or bad, obedient or foolish. But that's not what we've been discussing in these past few paragraphs. Our experience in this world will be one of iterative growth, where we take steps of obedience followed by missteps of sin—whether willful or habitual or fully unconscious.

It's Paul's observation that gives us hope because he reminds us that the law of the Spirit of life is greater than the law of sin and death. Our forgetful, disobedient missteps are already accounted for in the sacrifice of Jesus. But that doesn't discount the wisdom of what James is trying to tell us. A constant rehearsal of the truth that we've settled in the previous pages is a necessary exercise in the process of sanctification. That's why James says that we are not only to look at the perfect law of liberty, but we are also to continue in it. It's the continual march forward that produces maturity in the life of a disciple. It's the agreement to be a doer and not just a hearer that leads to the blessed life.

We began our conversation by establishing that Scripture is a reliable source of eternal truth. We continued that discussion by looking at what Scripture says about God—and what God says about anyone who is in Christ. We did our best to use models as effective tools for understanding how we allow the life of Jesus to pass through us to display His love for the world around us. And we offered up the idea that we might

be more accurately defined as Saints who are still subject to the influence of sin rather than sinners saved by grace.

The days ahead are filled with choices about what we'll do with that information. Will we continually rehearse the volume of identifying verses about anyone who is in Christ, or will we simply find the information in the short book interesting—and then walk away from the mirror forgetting what sort of person we are? May God give us the grace to choose the former.

Take heart. Just like the infant taking his or her first steps, the road ahead can be challenging as we learn a new spiritual equilibrium. Coming to grips with the truth of who we are in Christ can be as disorienting as anything we've ever experienced. When you find yourself living out the same habits that have been the hallmark of your younger existence, remember our discussion of the Greek actors. You are only a hypocrite when you are acting contrary to the definition that God has declared to be true about you. Find a handful of defining Scriptures about who you actually are and say them to yourself again and again as a corrective step that guides you away from the filthiness and wickedness that James says we are to lay aside.

Finally, remember that it's not perfect performance that confirms your faith in the God-given identity you've been provided through Jesus. The fact that you are even trying to live in holiness is the evidence that your heart has been made new and you desire what God desires. Remember that growth comes in the stumbling and the struggle, but only if we choose to recognize that God gives us the strength to stand when we fall and try again when we fail. Accepting the identity of a saint of God is the first step in the process of being made new, but it's far from the only step.

As you bring your time in this book to a close, I would strongly recommend that you quickly start working your way through *Narrow Gate Notes on Purpose*. As we stated in the opening of this book, this course of study is taught in four sections: Scripture, Sainthood, Sanctification, and Servanthood. We've taken time to settle our minds regarding the reliability of Scripture and the truth of who we are in Christ (sainthood). Now it's time to learn how we begin the process of sanctification as we are transformed, more and more, into the image of Jesus. And, as we dive deeper into how that transformation takes place, we'll discover the general purpose for anyone who bears the name of Jesus, and the specific purpose or role you play in the life of service to the God who made you and the world He seeks to save.

Father, give us the grace to believe and act on the truth that You have allowed us to see. Keep our hearts filled with joy and our minds filled with hope, as we walk out the life that You have ordained for us to live. Remind us that our truest view of self is always found when we stare into the mirror of your truth, and our truest value is most fully known when we realize the price that Jesus paid to reconcile us to You. Empower us to love and live as You loved and lived in Christ. It's in His name that we ask this prayer. Amen.

Let's Connect

Narrow Gate is a place where young men can quiet the distractions of everyday life and discover a life that matters, but it's also a community where people of all ages find purpose in supporting the mission of the organization.

Consider this your invitation to be a part of our family. Whether you're a young man who is considering becoming a student or a friend or family member who knows someone who would benefit from this experience, we invite you to:

- Follow us on Instagram @narrowgatelodge
- Follow us on Facebook @narrowgatefoundation
- Subscribe to our YouTube channel at Narrow Gate Foundation
- Shop our goods made for life at narrowgateleather.org
- Purchase our specialty fresh roast at narrowgate.coffee
- Help transform lives by transforming your home with our real wood beams, mantels, floating shelves and more at tnboxbeams.com
- Sign up for our email newsletters, request a Narrow Gate speaker, schedule a tour, or connect with our staff at info@narrowgate.org or 931-583-0633.

The eight-month residential experience at Narrow Gate Lodge is available to qualified young men, regardless of their financial resources. We have been able to offer students tuition-free experiences since our inception because of the generosity of thousands of people—and we invite you to join us. Narrow Gate is a 501(c)(3) nonprofit and donations are tax deductible.

Would you or your organization like to make a contribution or receive additional information?

Please contact us at:

931-583-0633

office@narrowgate.org

P.O. Box 267, Duck River, TN 38454

Are you a young man between the ages of 18 and 25 who would like to apply?

Learn more at:

nglodge.org